England) Savage Club (London, Andrew Halliday

The Savage-Club Papers

England) Savage Club (London, Andrew Halliday

The Savage-Club Papers

ISBN/EAN: 9783743306721

Manufactured in Europe, USA, Canada, Australia, Japa

Cover: Foto ©ninafisch / pixelio.de

Manufactured and distributed by brebook publishing software (www.brebook.com)

England) Savage Club (London, Andrew Halliday

The Savage-Club Papers

Preface.

IN the preface to the volume of *Savage-Club Papers* published last year, it was stated that the purpose of the book was to assist the widow of an artist.

I am happy to be able to report that our efforts were successful. The money obtained by the sale of the *Papers* was placed in the hands of Mr. Tom Hood and Mr. Jonas Levy, gentlemen whose names will be a full guarantee for its security and proper application.

It is most gratifying to us to know that the aid we have been enabled to offer in this case has been effectual.

Lest anyone should require a reason to be given, other than is to be found in the book itself, why we publish a second series of *Savage-Club Papers*, I reply: Our publisher, Mr. Tinsley, being particularly well satisfied with our last volume, *asked* for a second series.

Having given this reason, authors, at least, will

say, there is no necessity to mention any other. But I may as well state candidly all the considerations which weighed with us in the scale of decision.

Although there was no present demand upon our efforts, we had reason to fear that appeals might soon be made to us. We deemed it better, therefore, to take the opportunity offered us of forming a Fund, from which claimants might be assisted if occasion should arise, than to risk emergencies which might find us unprepared.

The last consideration had more weight with us than all the others. By publishing the *Papers* every year—which, with the favour of the public, it is our intention to do—we hope to render assistance to our unfortunate brethren without parading their names and calling public attention to their distresses.

But we desire most expressly to state that we appeal to no one's charity. Here is the book. Let it stand upon its own merits.

No more need be said, except that the Poetry, Prose, Music, and Pictures which form this volume are contributed gratuitously, and that we are again indebted to Mr. E. C. Barnes for superintending the illustrations of the work.

THE EDITOR.

Contents.

	PAGE
EXCEPTIONAL EXPERIENCES. By T. W. Robertson	1
THE HOUR-GLASS. By W. Sawyer	9
A BORDER RAID IN 1867. By Godfrey Turner	14
THE LOST JEWEL. By J. R. Planché	31
LA FOSSE COMMUNE. By Walter Thornbury	33
HOLDING THE CANDLE. By Andrew Halliday	47
ADAPTING FROM THE FRENCH. By John Hollingshead	57
MY ULTIMATUM. By H. S. Leigh	62
BEGOTTEN OF SAD STARS. By the Author of "The Waterdale Neighbours"	64
THE RAVEN. By John Oxenford	86
TERRIBLE TELEGRAMS. By Thomas Archer	88
MRS. RALPH GREENING'S FIRST LODGER. By Arthur Locker	100
THE VISION IN THE WOOD. By Westland Marston	118
ARTEMUS WARD AMONG THE SHOSHONES. By Edward P. Hingston	124
THE MAGICAL OINTMENT. By Hain Friswell	140
ST. ANTHONY'S SERMON. By Walter Thornbury	155
BILGER'S. By G. M. Fenn	158
A CHRISTMAS FAIRY. By H. J. Byron	176

	PAGE
CHARACTERS AND SCENES. By Edward Draper	178
A VISIT TO THE PRESIDENT OF THE EARLY RISING ASSOCIATION. By George Grossmith	186
MUSIC. By German Reed	195
DEALINGS WITH THE DEVIL. By Sutherland Edwards	203
A SCRAP FROM A COMEDY. By Dion Boucicault	211
BILL BANKS'S DAY OUT. By "The Journeyman Engineer"	214
THE LAST BIRTHDAY RHYME. By Mortimer Collins	231
STEAMBOATING IN AMERICA. By Howard Paul	233
THE DEVIL-TREE. By James Greenwood	241
THE TIME WILL COME. By Frank Younge	255
THREE HUNDRED AND FOUR. By G. A. Sala	259
THE POWER OF MUSIC	274
UNCOMFORTABLE PEOPLE. By W. Kirkus	275
LOVE'S SEASONS. By W. Brough	284
A "MODEL" CHILD. By E. C. Barnes	286
HOW THE GHOST WALKED. By H. Leslie	292
BUCKINGHAM GATE	302

ILLUSTRATIONS.

	Artist	
FRONTISPIECE	W. Brunton.	
TITLE-PAGE	Harry Rogers.	
THE TRYST	G. Thompson	*To face p.* 8
GIOVANNA	E. C. Barnes	31
HOLDING THE CANDLE	W. Brunton	47
THE TELEGRAM	J. Palmer	88
A VISION IN THE WOOD	Isaac Brown	120
ST. ANTHONY PREACHING TO THE FISHES	W. Brunton	155
CENDRILLON	Gustave Doré	177
AN OLD BOY	Edward Draper	179
THE LAST ROSE OF SUMMER	D. T. White	184
LOVE'S SEASONS	E. Hull	195
FAITHFUL UNTO DEATH	Harrison Weir	202
BETWEEN TWO TRAINS	George Cruikshank	211
A HUMAN WAIF	J. Palmer	224
A BIRTHDAY RHYME	E. C. Barnes	231
FALLING LEAVES	Alfred Slader	241
WATER-BABIES	G. S. Walters	255
CATCHING DABS	F. Barnard	259
THE POWER OF MUSIC	Charles Morgan	274
A "MODEL" CHILD	E. C. Barnes	286
BUCKINGHAM GATE	John O'Connor	302

Engraved by DALZIEL BROTHERS.

THE SAVAGE-CLUB PAPERS.

Exceptional Experiences.

BY T. W. ROBERTSON.

I REGRET to have to appear before the public, for I am a modest and retiring person. My name is De Jones; and, if I may be allowed the expression, not only is my name Jones, but my nature is Jones too—eminently so. I am a very commonplace man; I never did anything to distinguish myself; I never wanted to; I never will. I endeavour to be as like my fellow-creatures as possible; my desire is to be in the ruck—in the rank and file. I therefore esteem it a particular hardship that nothing should happen to me as it happens to other people—that I am doomed, fated, and condemned to see, feel, hear, taste, and smell everything exceptionally. Let me explain. Either everybody in the past and in the present time has misrepresented everything, or I see persons and things through a perverted and jaundiced medium. Which is it? Is all the world untruthful, or am I mad or a hypochondriac or an idiot, or all three? But to my experiences.

I once went to Ireland, where I believe it to be an understood thing that all carmen are witty. I lived in Ireland a year, during which period of time I took several cars, and conversed with several carmen. I will take my oath before any justice of the peace that I never heard any one carman utter anything approaching to a witticism. I never heard or saw a carman say or do anything that exhibited a sense of humour. A duller set of dogs I never met. One London cabman has more fun in him than all the car-drivers from Ballinafad to Ballinasloe, wherever those places may be.

Conscious of the fate to which I am doomed, I inquired of other persons who were in the habit of taking cars whether *they* had ever, with their own ears, heard a Dublin or any other Irish carman say a clever thing. As I expected, there was no authentic instance upon record. The witticisms put into the mouths of Irish carmen are the ingenious inventions of Messrs. Charles Lever, Samuel Lover, William Carleton, and other educated men.

Who has not laughed at the famous engraving in *Punch*? A stranger in the mining districts is passing two colliers. One collier, after hearing from his mate that the individual in question is not a native of those parts, says, " Heave a half-brick at him!"

I once went into the mining districts. What were my experiences? I was treated not only with consideration and courtesy, but with attention and kindness.

I was walking in the Black Country, and I had lost my way. I was tired and hungry. It was somewhere near a place called Willeshall or Willesley, and the road, or rather footpath, was all up and down and in and out. I asked several of the miners whom I met to direct me to a certain Victoria Hotel, where I had been told I could dine well. Instead of replying to me with their doubled fists between my eyes, or offering to fight me for a quart of beer, the men answered me civilly, and in two or three instances went out of their way to show me the road. However, the Victoria Hotel was not to be found, and I was fain to turn into a road-side public-house called the Three Furnaces, where the landlady cooked me a rasher of excellent ham, placed a large cheese before me, with the addition of beer and grog; offered and furnished me with slippers for my feet, because I looked weary; and when I asked for the bill, charged me—*ninepence*. On my objecting to the charge as ridiculously small, she and her husband said that the week before some inspectors had made the same remark; but that, for their part, they did not like to impose upon strangers.

I have been in seaport-towns; I have seen men-of-war paid off; I have been at sea; but I never saw a jolly sailor: and yet one would think that Smollett and Mr. Tom Dibdin and Captain Marryatt must have known. I can only speak to the fact. Seamen are *not* jolly. When a damp misanthropic-looking mate stamps on the deck and utters incoherent cries, and three uncomfortable, unwashed men emerge from a dank cabin, they, the men or watch, do not come up smiling; they appear to be in lower spirits than a sawyer at his pit or a bricklayer with his trowel.

I was once in the Channel on a Saturday, and I resolved to pass a roaring evening, toasting sweethearts and wives with the men for'ard. I scraped acquaintance with a seaman, an open-hearted tar, who took my half-crown grimly, and he introduced me to the fore-cabin, where he told me the evening was to be devoted to singing, to the cheerful glass, and general harmony. "Huzza!" thought I. Dibdin for ever! "The Wooden Walls of Old England," "Three cheers for the Red, White, and Blue," "We Tars have a maxim, your Honour, d'ye see," &c. &c.—mirth, music, muscle, manhood, and Captain Marryatt!

The roof of the cabin was so low that you could not sit upright, but had to keep your chin about four inches from your knees, in a position more calculated to promote curvature of the spine than good fellowship or conviviality. It was quite dark. There was not any air, but there was plenty of smoke. As I descended, an able-bodied seaman was having a most violent row with his messmates about a teaspoon. He reflected on their honesty in terms even stronger than the flavour of tobacco that impregnated what should have been the atmosphere. At last he swore himself down, and the fun began.

One low-spirited sailor sang a low-spirited love-song in a deep bass voice. The first verse ran:

> "A marchant-man he lived in Hull,
> He had a daughter—only gal,
> She was most beauti-ful and fair;
> And she fell in love with a jolly tar.
> Whack-fal-dee-du-di-day,
> Whack-fal-dee-du-di-day!"

Then every dispirited seaman droned out, in doleful chorus:

> "Whack-fal-dee-du-di-day,
> Whack-fal-dee-du-di-d-a-y!"

This cheerful chant, the economically sung chorus included, lasted about three quarters of an hour, and was succeeded by another mirth-inspiring ditty, that also treated of the gay subjects of shipwreck and disaster, with a hundred tons burthen of—

"Tow-row-row!
Lay along now!
Be handy, boys, be handy, O!"

How long this song continued I know not, for I escaped to the moonlit deck, thinking to myself, If these be sailors at sea in their hours of hilarity, what must they be in their moments of misery?

But enough of my exceptional experiences, for I have to mention another shortcoming which I regret extremely; but I cannot help it. I have a friend—let us call him S. Myth, who has recently risen in the world, and, to avow the truth, I like him now as well as I did before he had achieved a reputation.

In hearing S. Myth spoken of among his friends and acquaintance, it is wonderful how his faults and vices have come uppermost since his success. He used to be considered a decent fellow, with plenty of faults and a few good qualities, in short an average kind of man; but now I hear, that when a boy he stole apples and preserves, fought his younger brother, slapped his little sister, and at the earliest age gave evidences of precocious villany. The other day I met a mutual friend of mine and S. Myth's, and as I was remarking that I had great pleasure in observing S. Myth's rise in the world, I was surprised by our mutual friend bursting out with:

"And are you—*you*, De Jones—so dazzled by that man's success, that you are blinded to the fact of his being an utter impostor—a mere fluker and a thorough cad? Why, the man has no merit whatever; and he is so inflated by his luck that there is no coming near him!"

I said that I was sorry to hear that; but that I myself had not observed any difference in his manner.

"You must be blind," replied my and S. Myth's mutual friend. "The fellow is such a horrid ruffian. Don't you know that he poisoned his own mother?"

This startled me, and I said that it was the first I had heard of it, that I had not thought success could have so far intoxicated him, and that I considered that a man who could poison his own mother was not only guilty of a great imprudence, but must be devoid of every honourable sentiment and reciprocal feeling.

"S. Myth," said our mutual friend, "is capable of anything."

"But," I objected, "he can't have poisoned his mother, for I dined with her three days ago."

"The old lady has a very strong constitution, and it resisted the effects of the strychnine."

"But," I urged, "she seemed perfectly good friends with her guilty son."

"You know what mothers are."

I always think that the person who is speaking is in the right, so I said, "Yes; the more you poison them, the more they forgive you."

"Just so."

"Still," I continued, "I do not believe that, with all the bad qualities that success engenders in the human heart both before and after its accomplishment, S. Myth could have gone so far."

Our mutual friend smiled a derisive smile, and said, as he walked away:

"De Jones, I am sorry."

"For what? For S. Myth's rascalities?"

"No; but that his success blinds you to them!"

I felt I was a sycophant; but still my nature is adhesive, and I like S. Myth, and I will not believe all I hear against him, though every day I am told that he keeps on poisoning his mother. What a wonderful constitution the old lady must have!

Gordon Thompson, del.   Dalziel Bros., sc.

THE TRYST.

The Hour-Glass.

BY WILLIAM SAWYER,

Author of "Ten Miles from Town," &c.

THE sea-green moonlight fills the cell
   Wherein, at midnight, prays alone
A kneeling Brother, lank and lean,
   And still as carven out of stone.

High, where the three-feet wall is pierced,
   Against a lancet-window, leaps,
Swinging in gusts, a vine—and near
   A squinting gargoyle slily peeps.

Before the Image of our Lord
   A pictured Missal open lies,
Its wrought initials burnish'd gold,
   Its column'd words in blending dyes.

Beside the book, an hour-glass set,
　　Half in its oaken frame conceals
Two shining bubbles, lightly blown,
　　Through which the sand-thread redly steals.

Not on the Image of the Lord—
　　Not on the Missal's dazzling blaze;
But on the red sand's wasting thread
　　The kneeling Brother bends his gaze.

To turn that glass from hour to hour,
　　Throughout the day, throughout the night;
He makes the duty of a life
　　Which heaven, he deems, has shaped aright.

And ever as the glass he tends,
　　His hungry eyes of God beseech
That light of Grace He will bestow,
　　Or grains of saving wisdom teach.

"Dear Christ," he cries, "perchance Thy feet
　　Thou on this desert sand hast set;
Each grain Thy tear-drops have bedew'd—
　　Thy agony of blood has wet.

It knew Thee not—it knows not now
　　The part that hour by hour it plays:
Marking the bounds of work and rest,
　　Of steadfast prayer, of eager praise.

And I!—what know I of the ends
   That we in Thy creation serve?
What boots the right when we are true,
   Or what the evil when we swerve?

Of Thy good purpose in our lives
   (Or ignominious or sublime)
We dream as little as the sand
   Dreams that it marks the flight of time."

No more. On either globe, a star,
   The sea-green moonlight shimmers white:
He sees it not, or sees as one
   Who gazes through some inner light.

But when the hour is done, and while
   There flickers down the last red grain,
He starts out of his dreams, and turns
   The glass—and, hark, his voice again!

"Dear Lord," he cries, "this desert sand
   Surely interprets Thee to-night!
For, while the Missal glimmers dim,
   Its every sparkle glows with light.

The secret mysteries of life
   My eyes are quicken'd to discern;
Nor less, as thus I gaze and muse,
   The golden laws of duty learn.

I mark that on its destined way
  The stream in order'd cadence goes:
Unhasting, but unceasing, still
  Without a sound it flows and flows.

Whether Thy solemn Word it mete,
  Or measure out a mortal strain,
It heeds not, questions not, but falls
  In rhythmic beauty, grain on grain.

Let a Saint's fingers grasp the glass,
  Or Judas hold it in his hand,
Nor one nor other may retard
  Or quicken the insensate sand.

' So go thou thine appointed way,'
  It seems to murmur to my soul :
' Achieve the purpose of a life
  Whereof thou seest not the whole.

' Whatever gird thee round about,
  Of seeming good or seeming ill,
Do thou thy duty : what befals
  It is for God, not thee, to will.' "

The blue lips cease : but musing on
  He wrestles with the growing thought,
Until the shaven temples throb,—
  There where a net the veins have wrought.

The night wears out.   The moon goes down,
   The vine to fresher gusts is swung,—
And, lo! the squinting gargoyle thrusts
   From its stone mouth a stony tongue!

A Border Raid in 1867.

BY GODFREY TURNER.

—o—

IT must, I fear, be owned that the Melrose district has been, of all the length and breadth of the Scottish Border, the most thoroughly explorated, cockneyfied, and pumped-out; seeing that, whatever else of interest the holiday-raider in that region may be compelled or tempted to pretermit, he on no account fails to "do" his Abbotsford, his Dryburgh Abbey, and his yet more indispensable lunar expedition to "St. David's ruined pile" in the valley of Melrose, under tricuspid Eildon. But might it not betray a vulgar weakness if any one should affect to see vulgarity in a visit to Melrose by moonlight, or to Abbotsford in those hours of daytime which are set apart for the show? Shakespeare is not vulgar, for all the "revivals" he has undergone, nor because of the blunders and bickerings of his commentators, nor from his having been trimmed down into "Beauties" by Parson Dodd. Liberty is not vulgar, whatever may be said or done in her name and to her disparagement at a Demonstration.

I will, notwithstanding, make a clean breast of my intentions in a recent Border raid, and confess that, when I lately started northward on this journey of perfunctory enjoyment, I had the smallest possible care to see the lions that are so glowingly depicted in the guide-books—that are described, I say, by letter-press and wood-cut as well as by the keepers who show them at a trifling charge. Though I yield to nobody in an admiring love of Sir Walter Scott's genius, I am little interested in his trousers, waistcoat, and gloves. Out of the beaten track, to the west far of Melrose and of Selkirk and Galashiels, and beyond the vales of Ettrick and Yarrow, and away from Selkirkshire entirely, and past the southernmost point of Peeblesshire, and into the county of Dumfries, the Rasselas of a railway-era must roam to find the Happy Valley. It is Eskdale.

Of Eskdale, and of "its pleasant little capital of Langholm, charmingly situated amidst woods, waters, and hills," I had, while staying on a short visit near Kelso, a singularly appetising account in a letter which was addressed to me by "A Borderer;" and I take this public occasion to say, privately, that I have lost this gentleman's card,

if I ever had it; and that it would give me very
great pleasure to know "A Borderer's" real name.
Time did not permit me to see Langholm; but I
put into practice a few of the kindly hints which
were offered me in respect of "classic Yarrow,"
taking Selkirk on my way through that valley of
diamonds to St. Mary's Loch. Had it not been
for my unknown friend's valuable suggestions I
might never have gone to look upon St. Mary's
Loch, and to shake hands with the historic Tibbie
Shiel, who survives by many years the generation
of sportsmen and wits, and poets and scholars,
by whom her name has been bequeathed as a
household word to our children. St. Mary's
Loch, a curving sheet of water, about three miles
and a half long and not quite a mile broad, is
separated by just a narrow neck of land from the
Loch of the Lowes, the "lake of lakes," another
and a smaller gem of placid, winsome beauty, set
amid the strength of the everlasting hills. But,
in spite of its undeniable charms and its flattering
etymology of title, the Loch of the Lowes will not
sustain comparison with "sweet St. Mary's Loch,"
which is so grandly girt about by massive shapes
that, for all its great superiority in point even of
mere size over the Loch of the Lowes, it seems
only "a dew-drop on the lion's mane." This
pearl of pools, this baby lake, that sleeps as still
as peace, held in the hollow of a great hand, is

surely as perfect a symbol of rest as the weary
suppliant of that renewing power could, in a
simple pleasure-jaunt, hope to see. Various indeed
are the aspects of the solitary mountain-
mirror; various as the hours and seasons that
look on it while they pass—that are reflected in
it—that float double on its bosom, like the swans.
But the same lone, modest loveliness, I fancy,
must be always there. It is the loveliness of the
violet half hidden under the mossy stone—of the
one star, " when only one is shining in the sky."
What though, in strict verity, it has neighbours
and rivals? St. Mary's Loch is yet peerless and
alone—*in* their company, it is true, but not *of* it.
You forget all without, when you have entered
the magic circle that contains so compact and harmonious
a picture. It was late in the year now
going out, it was in the last days of salmon-fishing
and the first of falling leaves and fur waistcoats,
when I took a long day's jaunt from Selkirk, to
see what I should see 'twixt that thriving Scoto-
Saxon burgh and the picturesque waterfall known
fantastically as the Gray Mare's Tail. It was late
in the year, I say, but not injuriously late for my
journey. The sedge had not withered from the
lake; neither had birds ceased to sing. The diamonds
strung on the gossamer had not changed
their sparkle for the lack-lustre clamminess of
clouded paste; the gold of the woods was not

quenched in an untimely "regret of the sun." The hill-tops round St. Mary's Loch, it is true, were veiled by a Scotch mist that morning; but the folds were lifted one by one, baring all the beauties they had covered from sight; and even while those folds remained, or were but tardily unrolling, or were thickened again, layer on layer, just as you expected the last one of all to be drawn up, there was a charming continuity of variable, fluctuating loveliness, that can neither be imagined by nor described to the prejudiced experience which confuses a Scotch mist with a Cheapside fog. I should be exceedingly loth, indeed, to lose the impression derived from that sight of St. Mary's Loch, which was one moment a glimpse, and the next moment less than that, and the next a dim and uncertain wakening of the scene, like the struggle of a melody to be remembered, and then a *crescendo* of brightness finishing with the full burst of a grand harmonious vision. I would peremptorily refuse to change this recollection of the mountain loch, let me at once declare, for the bluest and sunniest ideal of an ornamentally romantic pool, in the meridian warmth of a "fine day;" such as we contemplate amid the gentle hopes of a pic-nic on Virginia Water.

Selkirk, my point of departure for the Yarrow and Ettrick vales, and St. Mary's Loch, and the Gray Mare's Tail—a journey over more than fifty miles of ground, or I am mistaken—is a breezy town to which you ascend by a steep winding road from the railway-station. If your advent be after sunset, and there happen that night to be no visible moon or stars, you ought not to feel astonished at having to proceed through total darkness to the hotel on which your choice is bent. There are no lamp-posts in Selkirk, and there are no lamps to light the outer ways. There is gas, if my memory be not treacherous on this point, inside some of the houses; for I now bethink me of having with my own hand illumined my sitting-room, at the hotel, by means of sulphuretted-hydrogen, jetting from a showy modern piece of brass-work and painted porcelain and figured glass, in the midst of the chamber. But outwardly there is thick and threefold Stygian gloom, as black as ever the night may chance to be. Selkirk is yet worth your tarrying to see by daylight. It is fortunate, like other Border towns which might readily be named, in having advanced in practical importance without losing the pristine interest and beauty of its situation. It boasts, indeed, few historical relics; the most dearly prized, perhaps, being an English standard brought away from Flodden Field. On that fatal plain, if " the flowers of the forest were a' wede awa," the lowly craftsmen of Selkirk, those far-famed " souters wha sewed the single-soled shoon," made a more effectual as well as an equally courageous stand against the stubborn English foe. The Selkirk men, like the men of Hawick, came off conquerors in detail, though sharers in the aggregate defeat; sharers in the heaviest burden of consequent suffering, moreover; for the English, exasperated by the fierce resistance of those cobbling knaves, who would *not* understand the limit of their vocation, but travelled absurdly beyond their last, laid waste the little town with fire. It grew up again, and must, I fancy, have been a neat, substantial sort of place rather more than a century and a quarter afterwards, when Montrose and his victorious troopers found rest, one September night, and stabling for their horses, within the town, while the foot-soldiers were left to bivouac on Philiphaugh below. Then it was that the loyal marquis, after having six times defeated the English army, exposed himself to a disaster that sent him sorely stricken over wild trackless Minchmoor, to hide himself again in old Highland sanctuaries. In just such a Scotch mist, and on just such a September morning, as this holiday reminiscence of mine discloses, the English general, Sir David Leslie, who had been sent to seek out Montrose after the battle of Naseby, and to crush him, stole silently upon Philiphaugh and upon the astonished soldiery there encamped. It was a brief and desperate struggle, that ended in the flight of Montrose with a handful of followers. A monument stands on the spot where he was beaten; and two miles further up the Yarrow, in the vicinity of Newark Castle, is a field grimly named the Slain Man's Lea, it being here that — tradition saith — Sir David's soldiery despatched many of their prisoners, a day or two after the battle.

To speak of even a mere three-weeks' scamper to and fro and up and down in the inexhaustible Border-country is a hard matter for the most methodical of scribbling tourists. However fast in the flesh your journey may have been, the ground is, morally and reflectively speaking, ground that you cannot hurry over. The more haste you attempt to make, the worse decidedly is your speed. At every step—to repeat a formula which is almost trite among Borderers—you will be apt to break your shins against history; and a halt for the length of half a page at least becomes needful, that you may rub the contusion. Perhaps the ointment readiest to your hand will be something from the Waverley pharmacopœia; perhaps it will be such medicament as you are like to find in those wild-flowering simples, the old Border ballads; or you may comfort your bruise with balm borrowed from True Thomas of Ercildoun; or it will content you to apply soothingly a few leaves from Fuller or Leland, or from David Hume of Godscroft, or from Nicholson, or from any of the authorities cited by Bishop Percy, or from Thingumy's History of the Scottish Border. For my own part, look you, I derived much assuagement, in all such circumstances, from those later volumes of Mr. Froude's—I had, by a lucky impulse, crammed them into my travelling-bag, detrimentally to the smoothness of my chiefest shirts, as I was about leaving Kelso—which thoughtfully discourse of Mary Stuart.

Before visiting Selkirk, I was for a day's space at Jedburgh, and made a morning call at a low-roofed house in a back street, and saw the room wherein the Queen of Scots lay sick, nigh unto death, of the fever she caught of that strange mad ride of forty miles to see her wounded favourite at Hermitage Castle. The thick walls, the low-beamed chambers, the small window-sockets, the narrow winding stair of stone, all the solidly-integrant parts, in short, of this mansionling, denoted to us a date well back in the Tudor period. "Us" were four gentlemen, of whom not one had ever entered the house until that day; and I fear that the bland and almost courtly politeness of our spokesman—the most determined explorer in the party, by the bye—scarcely atoned for our unrelenting curiosity, insatiable as it was until we had examined every corner from garret to kitchen. I have said that substantially the house we thus invaded was a Tudor house; but as much as could be done to modernise the interior of the inhabited rooms, without altering the constructive character of those apartments—which, indeed, would have been an all but impossible feat, so strong and massive was the original building—had been accomplished. The standard of living would not now tolerate as fit and suitable for a decent mechanic's family that which sufficed for a queen and her court three centuries ago. The great historical essayist who has written, in our day, better than most of his predecessors, concerning those times of Elizabeth and of Mary Stuart, remarks that the captive queen in her cage, in the round tower of Lochleven Castle—where it is only " to be hoped" that the narrow slit in the wall, which served for a window, was protected by glass; where, in lieu of stairs, the ascent to her circular room was made by means of a ladder, through an opening in the floor; where " decency must have been difficult, and cleanliness impossible"—had about the same allowance of comfort which fell to other dames in the stern rough feudal time; so, too, I think, in that quaint house of dark chambers which a tall man must stoop to stand in, of darker passages, and strait steep flights of winding stairs, Queen Mary's convalescence should have been well nigh as ill a thing as her terribly dangerous disease. We went into the topmost rooms, which, being disused, retain their olden appearance, or, rather, show in their age what they must have been when they were young. When they were young! I saw, in one of those upper rooms, spread out upon the worm-eaten oak floor, a piece of curious needlework, from whose crowned figures of kings and queens, and from whose brass-mailed warriors, of Scripture story, the colours had gone clean out. Robes and vests and turbans, cinctures and anklets of gold, trinkets of sapphire and ruby and emerald and every precious stone in his kind, had come at last to the single complexion, the ultimate flesh-tint, dust. There was indeed one loitering hue, one impertinent pigment, a moderately bright indigo, which had refused to budge. Ridiculous emblem of vain antiquity! To what purpose wilt thou freshen with azure that sandal, or the folds of that tunic, or the zenith of that sky in which the sun is a round pallid phantom of a mass of clay? Thou art, in truth, dead, dead as an old man whose companions are all "sleeping away the child's-play of life," and who alone remains of the band, foolishly supposing that he lives.

The whole Border-country, as I take it, is a great kirk-yard full of green graves and gray memorial stones, and records on which Old Mortality loves to pore, the long summer-day. There is hardly a legend buried under the leaves of past years, in those quiet valleys, that has not a castle or an abbey for a head-stone. There is hardly an antique thorn, an oak, or a fir of decent growth, which does not afford some eloquent *hic jacet*. Melrose, you remind me, is vulgarised. True; I said so erewhile, cockney that I am. Nevertheless, I should have been vastly ashamed if I had neglected to visit the ruined Abbey, and by moonlight too. Of course I had in mind Sir Walter's famous recipe for seeing " fair Melrose aright;" though the best of the joke is, that he himself never saw the ruins by the light of the moon; and I was very anxious to ascertain the exact time of night when the reflected rays would fall upon broken arch, and shafted oriel, and ruined centre-tower. The moon, however, was scarcely due before eleven o'clock; so I went first to see the Abbey while my dinner was being prepared at the hotel, and, having gained access to the enclosure, and followed, with tame submission, the guide who told me all about this, that, and the other, I lingered in the adjacent churchyard, as the day sank to rest, and certainly saw the lovely ruin in a light at once appropriate and effective. The sun was dying, as regally as the poet might have fancied him to die, in blood without end, and gold without measure, and purple without stint. The glow that touched the crowns of the graceful pinnacles made sadder the solemn gray and the cold deepening shadows beneath. I question if moonlight could ever lay a gentler beauty on Melrose than this which dwelt awhile upon the crumbling spires, and then stole sadly away as the sinking splendour faded from the heaven. It is possible that, in taking this ground for a retrospect of my visit to Melrose, I may be influenced by a simple desire to find comfort for a certain disappointment which befel me, in respect of the brightness of the moon, that night. There were companions with me when I set forth a second time from the hotel. The moon was only a day or two past the full, and, though wreathed in haze when she had attained the requisite altitude, got almost clear of cloud for a minute or two—before being obscured again.

This tantalising sort of thing went on till our patience would no longer stand it. We could never, somehow, get the moon into focus. When she really might have been clear enough to glimmer feebly on the pinnacles and buttresses of the eastern end, she got provokingly behind the thick foliage of an elm ; and when she had sailed free of the boughs she grew misty again, or was blocked out entirely by a big mass of cloud. In fine, we lost the spell, became utterly indifferent to the situation, and talked in the most brilliant manner of the most commonplace things we could think of. Again and again I went to look on the ruins of elrose Abbey, while I was sojourning at Kelso

and in the neighbourhood; but I did not repeat
the moonlight expedition. It is pleasant to be
able to speak with praise of the care which is bestowed on these ruins; and to say, as one would
wish to say of everything and everybody, ancient
and venerable, that they are " provided for." The
turf is beautifully kept within the gray walls; and
the modest show of flowers, such as the monks
would have maintained trim and fresh in their
cloister walls, cannot be condemned as out of place
there. The stone of which the Abbey is builded is
so hard as to have retained in a wonderful manner
the most delicate touches of the monkish mason's
chisel; and the objects carven in the tabernacle
work, and on the pinnacles and arches, are of
endless fertility of design. The curling Scotch
kail is introduced not unfrequently; and a perfect
little gallery of stone pictures, leaf and flower, and
pilgrims' scollop-shell, all a-row in diaper squares,
adorns the cloister wall. The foliage on the capitals
of the pilasters, belonging to the entrance-door from
the cloisters, on the north side, is undercut with
such marvellous delicacy that a straw can be in-
terlaced through the work; and indeed I found
the long dry stalk of a blue-bell sticking there one
day, as it had been left by somebody who had
thus tested the fineness of the carving. The gargoyles, on all parts of the walls, are wonders of
invention, of skilful handiwork, and, for the most

part, of freshness. Many of them are as sharp and perfect as if chiselled yesterday. There is a galloping pig, which seems to start forward in violent action from below the roof, and which may have been meant to typify the swine that ran violently down a steep place into the sea. Another of these gargoyles, less perfectly preserved, is a representation of the blind man carrying the lame. Plants, animals, and human faces abound; the canny Scotch features of the rustic models having been, in several instances, done to the life. There is the likeness as plain as if you had the living head beside it. The churchyard grass, unlike that level turf which carpets the aisles of the ruined Abbey, is long and rank. A fragment of brown stone, lying amidst this herbage, bears one of the most eloquent and impressive epitaphs ever composed. It is in four lines, which run thus, without name or date or addition of any kind, but in lank thin letters like the skeleton sketch of a stone-cutter's inscription :

> " The earth goeth on, the earth glistening like gold :
> The earth goes to the earth sooner than it wold :
> The earth builds on the earth castles and towers :
> The earth says to the earth, All shall be ours."

As in fulfilment of its own solemn words, this admonitory stone seems to be sinking down into the earth, to whose very hue it has changed. Rotting brown mould; muffling cloak of green turf and ivy; sad gray walls and sadder evening sky—what place of pomp and pride and power have these taken? Banners that flaunted in bright colours and broidery of gold adown the richly lit aisles, full of incense and music, have left not a shred of their glory. Earl and Chieftain, Knight and Sage, Abbot and King, rise in pale imaging of the past, like the forms in a faded tapestry. "Is not earth indeed turned to earth, and shall not our sun set like theirs when the night comes?"

Holidays have a trick of ending. The right philosophy in which to pass them is the Epicurean —a total separation of the enjoyable present from the regretted past and the laborious future. But who is the traveller so determined and so bold that he can always prevent Black Care coming close behind and following him into the same compartment of the railway train? Our pleasant Border Raid is darkened towards the last by this unbeautiful shadow. There is no happiness, none, on the map that is crossed in all ways by railway lines. The period of the tourist's ticket has almost expired, and, just as we are beginning to feel ourselves Borderers bred, it becomes necessary to call for a Bradshaw, and to look out our time on the main line southward to Euston Square. So, we are soon rattling along on the iron road homeward. There is a pale early-morning look about everything as you wake up on your journey in the train that has been all the evening getting to Newcastle and all night getting past York; and the cup of existence tastes as if cigar-ashes had been dropped into it; and sunrise brings only headache; neither is there solace in boiling chicory; and the pork-pies and pastry are wearing green veils, and the refreshments generally are in deshabille; and the beautiful pink flush on the hooded face of the young lady sleeping in the farthest opposite corner of your carriage has all flown to her nose, where the tint ceases to be beautiful; and the wildness of your devotion to her and her luggage on the platform of the little Border-station, three hundred miles off, has by this time considerably toned down; and the only thing in life that will bear much thinking of is potash-water with a "wee drappie intil't;" and it's O, but breakfast will be a poor affair, I doubt, when you sit down to it, dazed and weary and limp and sad, in London.

E. C. Barnes, del. Dalziel Bros., sc.

GIOVANNA.

The Lost Jewel.

By J. R. Planché.

Wandering one day, I found
A diamond, Giovanna.
I had roam'd the world around
For that diamond, Giovanna!
Worth a monarch's diadem,
Princes envied me that gem—
Princes!—Ah!—Who envied them?—
Not I, Giovanna.

How I prized that precious stone!—
Kiss'd it, Giovanna.
A few brief months and it was gone!—
Lost, my Giovanna!
On another's hand it gleams,
With its sparkle pleased he seems;
But, alas! he little dreams
'Tis a diamond, Giovanna!

O, how much I envy him—
Him, my Giovanna!
Let but ought a moment dim
Its lustre, Giovanna,
From him lightly 'twould be tost,
Not one heart-pang him 'twould cost,
He would never *know* he lost
A diamond, Giovanna.

La Fosse Commune.

By WALTER THORNBURY.

IT was a flourish of trumpets that awoke me. It was evidently a regiment of cavalry passing down the Boulevard des Capucines.

My hotel was the Hôtel de Rochefort, at the end of the Rue de la Paix, the right-hand side as you come from the Place Vendôme; my bed-room was upon the first floor, and commanded a fine view of the Boulevard. I looked out, expecting to see nodding plumes, glittering helmets, perhaps the dancing particoloured flags of lancers, curvetting horses, glittering swords—a glimpse, at least, of that pomp and pageantry that hides the grinning skull and the gaping wound.

I opened the window and looked out. "Ventre bleu! Sacre bleu!"—*it was only Punch!* whose proprietor, having first planted himself and his tricolour show on a snug bare spot, near the garish new Opera House, had blown his trumpet defiantly, challenging all Paris to produce another such a Punch—a Punch more Mormon in tendencies, more imperially despotic in government, more bloodthirsty when in power, more crafty when in danger. No gendarme seized him, so he had not probably intended any satire on Goudinot, nor was that gay trumpet at all intended as a challenge to the Tuileries.

It was a fine September morning, so I remained in my "robe of night," looking out of the window in the direction of the Boulevard. The young trees were dressing slowly for death in the pale Bismarck colour, and as I looked, two dead leaves flew against the glazed hat of the driver of a fiacre, who, with a posy in his buttonhole, was stealing along the clean asphalte, just under my window, taking a bridal party to the Madeleine. The Napoleon Column was electro-plated with sun-light. It was as bright an autumn morning as ever shone on Paris. I thought upon illusions.

It was not the first Punch trumpet I had mistaken for that of a regiment of cavalry. That Chancery suit of mine was a Punch trumpet, as I found to my cost. That marriage of Sprodesbury with Miss Pendragon, the Carmarthenshire heiress, who turned out a "temper," that was Sprodesbury's Punch trumpet. Mr. Ruskin, one morning in Switzerland looked out of window and mistook a glass roof for a glacier. Life is full of such glass roofs, and every day Punch's trumpet leads some new gull into ruin.

Meditation made me hungry. Give me of the hot water, and I will myself shave. I shaved myself, I booted myself. I descended into the Sally Mangy, as Sprodesbury will call it, and I called three times, as in Arabian stories, "Louis! Louis! Louis!"

A Spaniard, a cold whiskery Englishman, and a newly-married couple from Tours, were already at breakfast. The Englishman regarded me—the senior resident in the house—the time-honoured frequenter of the Hôtel de Rochefort, with the cold superciliousness and parochial arrogance of his favoured nation. I heard him ask for eggs, which he called "*des yee*," but none of the waiters understood him, and I let him fret and redden and point and get angry, till at last they brought him a cutlet with garlic, and he went melancholy mad, refused breakfast, rushed to the Palais Royal, and that day left the hotel in despair.

Charles came to me, and dashed together with dexterous hand the brown coffee and the white warm milk.

"Where is Louis?" I asked.

"He is ill,—he has the grippe. You did not

dine at home yesterday, monsieur, or the day before, or you would have missed him. He has not been here since Monday."

"I was at the races at Charenton. I went on Saturday morning. I thought Louis then looked ill; but he said, no. You don't like Louis, Charles."

"*Tiens!* Yes; when we are not quarrelling. He is over me, you see, and he is so particular. But how he can cook an omelette! His father was *chef* at the Trois Frères, you understand. Yes, Louis is a *bon diable*, and will one day be head waiter."

Charles brought me my breakfast. When I had drank my first cup of coffee, and eaten my cutlet, and was waiting for my omelette with herbs, I strolled across the court-yard to the hotel door. The usual sights: dainty grisettes tripping past with bandboxes on their arms; close-shaved gentlemen bound for the Bourse; a soldier or two; a blouse or two; a street-boy singing a dance-tune from the opening of *Cendrillon;* a man in the road dripping water in a pleasant sprinkle across the legs and chest of a passing cab-horse; the Zouave sentinel at the Vendôme Column pacing fiercer and *chicier* than ever as an old soldier comes and puts a yellow garland of immortelles on the spiked rails of the demi-dieu, otherwise Scapin.

Drums at the corner of the Boulevard—real

drums, and a good many of them—muffled too; four black coaches—four more—then more drums. It is the funeral of a General, some relic of the Empire,—an old bit of steel broken at last, after being so often in the fire; coachmen in cocked hats, black cloaks, jack boots; portly, comfortable, cozy, well-dressed people in the carriages; in one vehicle extraordinary legal authorities in black and crimson gowns—some of them carry silver clubs and maces, and apparently fire-irons, and some wear strange coloured caps, like French prune-boxes.

Well, it never struck me before that people ever died in Paris. What! the city of pleasure—the glittering, gorgeous city, which lavishes its splendours out of doors, and does not hoard it so selfishly as London! What! the Paris of carnival, balls, and mad whirlpools of tipsy dancers—the Paris of incessant soldiers—the Paris of Napoleon and Paul de Kock—the Paris of cafés and theatres, and lamp-lit boulevards and squares of palaces! To die in Paris must be twice as much dying as dying anywhere else.

"*Qui va là?*" said an old soldier to a friend at the door of the hotel, and smiling grimly as he pretended to present arms.

"The old General Mouçard," said his friend. "*Prenez garde à vous.* Death is reading his muster-roll, and is getting near our names."

I turned back for my omelette. Charles was just emerging with it. He looked staggered and distressed. I heard him mutter "Louis."

"Is he better this morning?" I asked him instinctively.

Charles nodded his head gravely at a milk-jug; set down my omelette; a large tear fell on the edge of the plate as he answered slowly:

"*Monsieur, il est—mort!*"

Poor Louis!—so civil, so attentive, so chatty, so obliging and unmercenary. Did Death personally want a waiter, that he must needs ring our hotel bell and call imperatively "Louis!" —knowing—cruel—that from such a worthy fellow there could be but the one answer—"*Bien, M'sieu!*"

I inquired, and found that Louis, who rather pinched himself during his illness, not to distress his sister and niece with whom he lived, had sunk last night, about half-past eleven, from exhaustion. He was to be buried in thirty hours, as the law required. He was to be buried gratuitously—as all poor Parisians are—by the Company of the Pompes Funèbres: a very humble but respectable funeral, said Charles, and he should go, and take Mademoiselle Josephine—Louis's niece—the aunt was too old to go. The funeral would be in La Fosse Commune, Père la Chaise, to-morrow at three o'clock.

"La Fosse!—what?" I said, rather astonished at the phrase—"the common ditch!"

Charles replied gaily, that poor people like Louis were always buried in La Fosse Commune with many others; but their special graves were marked out and respected, and there was the proper funeral service that a good Christian Catholic could wish. It was the custom, and always had been the custom. His own father had been buried in that way, and he was delighted with the ceremony.

I determined to go and see poor Louis buried, and on the day named I strolled up the Rue de la Roquette, the scene of the miracle of the Zouave Guérisseur, and, passing the two prisons, safely reached the great entrance of Père la Chaise, in the dingy suburb over which it rears its miles of tombs.

I had no doubt now that the people of Paris did die. Miles of tombs—from the simple black cross to the stone barn that covers Napoleon's Marshals. Here and there, a bright fresh yellow wreath on the rails of a grave; here and there, autumn roses blooming palely but sweetly; but in how many of these stone sentry-boxes and little railed-in chapels forgetfulness and neglect, dusty tapestry of ragged cobwebs, rotting wreaths, broken plaster Virgins, shattered glass! "Regrets" —dirt, dust, and desolation! Forgotten—others now to fill the heart with fresh memories ; others by whom to be loved, and others to love! Love, come here and see where Love's resting-place is. I felt like Zimmerman in solitude, as I looked in dusty chapel after chapel, and heard the dead leaves crinkle under my feet like the dead ashes of Love's altar.

I stayed a moment to remove a cobweb from the bust of Balzac, and another moment to look down on Paris, with its domes and towers lying below,—a toy city, carved small in sapphire mist.

I asked one of the subordinate *croque-morts* following a girl's funeral (it looked like a wedding, for everyone was in white) the way to La Fosse Commune. He directed me to the side of the cemetery farthest from the entrance — a waste of half-neglected ground, as I thought—thistlely, rank, and purple with the careless blossoms of the wild geranium. The fellow left the funeral, and came sniffing after me for a franc. Miserable heartless hireling! he'd have stolen a body, if I had wanted it.

He brought me to a large waste ground, piled near the roadway with stacks of broken black crosses, broken marble slabs, and corroded pieces of zinc. The ground among the thistle and darnel and dock was strewn with every sort of votive offering and churchyard souvenir—glass, dishes of India-painted grass—representing angels leading away children, and widows under willow-trees, and widowers mourning over tombstones, with their faces hid in handkerchiefs — were there trampled to pieces, and rough with encrusted dirt. As for immortelles, they matted the ground in every stage of decay; some with the mere straw, others with a few beads left on them: many were fresh, as if only a few months out of the shop, and these the ghouls of Paris had kicked away among the nettles.

"And then," I said to the *croque-mort*, "what do the authorities do here?"

I saw at once what the ghouls had been doing, but I wanted to gauge the *croque-mort's* thimbleful of a heart.

"Monsieur," he said, removing his hat, "Messieurs the authorities clear the ground every six years, and these are the crosses of ladies and gentlemen buried here."

"And where to go to?"

Croque-mort smiled, took snuff, and shrugged his shoulders. I kicked a bunch of dock, and my foot came against a broken gilt-lettered slab. It was inscribed:

"FRANÇOIS PIERRE ARNAULD,
1861, aged 4 years.
And they brought unto Him little children, and He said,
Even so, for of such is the Kingdom of Heaven."

Only seven years, and now the grave is forgotten, the bones removed, and the tombstone broken into four pieces! The marble carving of that child's grave will form part of the next Fosse Commune.

Apropos of that, M. le Croque-mort, par exemple, where is La Fosse Commune? I move towards a franc in my waistcoat-pocket, and *croque-mort's* eyes twinkle with anticipations of absinthe. I take a last look on the stack of crosses, and the thistlely cemetery of bygone affections. Can this be Paris—the capital of a people who guard the frontier of civilisation — the people who hovered so long between despotism and liberty that they at last settled down on exactly what they did not want? But La Fosse Commune, I said to myself, that will be hallowed by the gorgeous ceremonials of an old religion. I can see clearly that, as Sterne said, "They do these things much better in France."

We came to the place in a dismal corner of the cemetery, on high ground, with an outlook across pleasant fields, and green ramparts, and rows of poplars. There was the Fosse—an enormous wide trench, some hundred and fifty yards long — a coarse rough trench, like a potato-pit, with the clay flung out in hills on either side. The Fosse I saw was newly opened, and had at present not more than thirty or forty inmates—that slope of loose earth hid them; and beyond that, two grave-diggers in their shirts rested on their spades waiting for another coffin. A long close regiment of black crosses, each with its simple yellow garland, marked the line of the last filled-up Fosse of buried Parisians. The priest, a tall, thin, almost imbecile old man, worn and poor-looking, wearing a not over-clean surplice, not longer than a spencer, and with a square pinched-up black cap on his head, sat near the Fosse on a chair; his acolyte, a stupid-looking shock-headed boy, in ordinary gamin dress, squatted near him, holding a brass *goupillon* or holy-water sprinkler in one hand, and a little wooden spade for throwing holy earth in the other. His eyes were steadily fixed on a large white butterfly that fluttered round a dandelion not far from where the priest sat. Presently I saw a coffin borne by two men on a black hand-bier. The coffin was a mere shell of thin deal —such as you see oranges packed in. The men in the glazed hats took out the coffin, and handed a small slip of paper to the boy, who gave it to the priest with one word, " *Homme.*"

The priest marked down the name on a card, as a guarantee of his fees, and wearily shook himself up for the service. I went up to the coffin—it was of unpainted and unplaned wood, and hardly closed on the joints, and on it was written, in large letters, " SOUFFLARD."

It was poor Louis; this was his ending!—and that hectic girl in ill-fitting black was Josephine,

his niece; that old woman—so portly, but yet
comfortable,—some good-natured neighbour. I
took off my hat, and approached the edge of the
Fosse. The coffin was lowered down into the
trench, and at once packed next the last comer—
quite close with a child's coffin—put endways, to
fill up the row. Two or three bystanders took off
their hats and ceased talking. Poor Josephine!
she wept bitterly, and clung to the old neighbour.
Ceremonials of the Church—jewelled dalmatics,
lighted torches, waving censers, cloth-of-gold
robes—where were they? I have buried a pet-
dog with more decency and ceremony than this.

 The old priest laid down his umbrella, and advanced book in hand. He read a Latin prayer—
some twenty times. You heard a monotonous
mumble of—*Qui es in cœlo*—*Benedictus*—*Magnifi-
cat*—*Amen*. The ill-favoured boy woke up at
Amen, and handed the *goupillon*. The priest
shook it on Louis's coffin, but no drop of water
came out of the sprinkler. The boy handed the
spade full of sand, the priest tossed it carelessly
towards Louis's coffin, but no grain of earth ever
touched it. The service was over; and as the
priest said the last *Amen*, and turned back to his
chair, his old faded umbrella under his arm, I heard
him say to the boy:

 "*Amen*. There was no water in the *goupillon*."

Poor Louis! no holy water had reached his coffin—no holy water to keep off the foul fiend. With such maimed rites are the poor of Paris buried!

There was an hysterical scream, and Josephine—her eyes red and sodden with weeping—forced her way through the wood of black crosses, which tore her gown as she broke through them—and threw herself on her knees, to take a last look at the coffin. The old woman followed, raised her, and comforted her.

There was no time for grief—another bier had arrived, and the grave-diggers were waiting with spades, ready for Louis's quiet neighbour. With horror and disgust I walked down the avenue, following slowly Josephine and her companion. As I approached them, a young man well dressed, but hot and angry, came up and spoke to them, and seeing me, took off his hat, and came towards me—it was Charles.

"Sacred pigs!" he said, "they told me at the office Louis was to be here at five, and, to make matters worse, they kept me cleaning knives just as I wanted to depart."

I pressed half a Napoleon into his hand. "Get a *fiacre*," I said, "and take home that poor girl, she seems faint—and give this other half to Louis's old aunt."

I walked slowly down the dirty avenue, and

so out of the pompous sham City of the Dead; just at the gate I heard somebody shout:

"Why, old man, who'd have thought of seeing you in Parry? Come and have a glass of bock at the 'Jolly Mourners,' as I have christened the *café* opposite."

It was Sprodesbury and a friend from Wales. We went and had a *chopine;* and as we discussed it, a *fiacre* drove by towards the Faubourg St. Antoine. The vehicle contained three people— Charles, Josephine, and the old woman. Charles had one of Josephine's thin hands in his, and his face was very near hers.

I said to myself, "There may some day be a marriage;" and then I thought of Louis, and—

"Out upon Time—that does but leave
Enough of the past for the future to grieve!"

"Why, what's the matter, old fellow?" said Sprodesbury, biting the tip off his cigar, "you seem rather down in the mouth. Come and dine at Vefours, and go and hear the Duchess of Gerolstein. Awfully jolly, let me tell you; and here, *gassvon*, von oter bock."

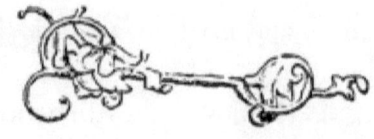

HOLDING THE CANDLE.

Holding the Candle.

BY ANDREW HALLIDAY.

THERE are a great many respectable people in the world who hold the candle to the devil, and think they are doing no great harm. Some of these hold the candle knowingly and with design, taking much pains to snuff and trim it, that the great artificer of mischief may have plenty of light to do his work by; but there are others who, though they would not willingly, and do not knowingly, assist such labours, are still morally guilty of the offence of holding the candle.

The unblushing candle-holder of the former class finds his lowest representative in the person who will not steal, but who will receive stolen goods, and his highest in the potentate who, by secret artifices, will set half the world by the ears in order to secure his own aggrandisement. The candle-holder of the latter class is the highly re-

spectable individual who, while he would scorn to
be a receiver of stolen goods, whether they are
silver spoons or provinces, will yet not refuse the
receiver's invitation to dinner. The moral guilt
of the person who tolerates the company of a fla-
grantly dishonest neighbour is obvious; but when
we substitute for the vulgar keeper of a fence in
Whitechapel the rich and powerful occupant of a
palace, the guilt of association is not so obvious;
but it is none the less great. Wealth, rank, influence, position, genius, notoriety even, are allowed
to hide a multitude of sins. The most respectable,
the most virtuous, the most conscientious of us, in
the hot pursuit of our honest ends, are constantly
giving countenance to unworthiness such as no
truly honest person ought to tolerate.

Between the fence in his dark and mysterious
cellar, and the emperor seated on his throne, we
shall find plenty of examples of candle-holding.
There is the poor but honest tradesman, struggling
to maintain a large family. He would scorn to do
a dishonest action; but he is not above taking the
hand of some neighbour whom he knows to be a
rogue. He will eat with him, drink with him,
deal with him, and accept favours at his hands
without scruple; his neighbour is a rogue, but his
ill-gotten money is as good and as clean as the
money of anyone else. In this class virtue is
constantly paying homage to vice. The mechanic,

who toils from morning to night at honest labour, looks up with admiration to the idle, dissolute, scampish betting man, whose gains enable him to wear fine clothes, and spend money lavishly in public-houses. There is nothing more pitiful than to see an honest, well-disposed, working-man dancing attendance upon a character of this kind; calling him "sir," humbly accepting his drink, laughing at his coarse and ribald jokes. Again, what could be more pitiful, more saddening to witness than the homage which virtuous women of the lower class pay to those shameless creatures of their own sex who are pleasantly named "gay ladies"? A humble, honest, virtuous woman of this class will work as cheerfully for one of these as she would for the most honourable lady in the land. She thinks it no shame to wait upon her in the humblest capacity; and if she wanted a companion, the poor woman would not scruple to send her one of her young daughters. Who has not seen poor, ill-clad, toil-worn mothers of families pause in the street to gaze with admiration, and almost longing, at some finely-dressed daughter of shame? The one redeeming quality of "gay" vice is generosity. There may, therefore, be some excuse for the honest poor in yielding suit and service to the sinner who sympathises with them — in holding the candle to one who is, in a very essential respect, *un bon diable*.

But this excuse vanishes gradually when we pursue our inquiries into higher spheres, vanishes until it disappears altogether. Poverty is a plea for many crimes, one that will often extenuate if not acquit. What shall we say of those who, urged by no necessity, stoop to hold candles to devils who are not good in any sense, who have no white spot about them, who are as black as any paint can make them, who willingly allow no one to share in the produce of their evil deeds? A familiar example of this devil is the successful City man. He is often of a low origin, one with whom, if he were not rich, no refined person would associate. He is often a vicious person, immoral and indecent in his way of life; one with whom, if he were not rich, no respectable person would willingly be seen. Yet, just because he is rich, refined persons forget his grossness, and respectable persons overlook his immorality. Honourable men are not ignorant that his wealth is acquired by transactions which will not bear the light of day; yet they flock to his table. Respectable mothers know that he is a *roué*, yet they trust their daughters in his company.

The worship of riches, even when adorned by virtue, is far from commendable. There are certain commoners, whom we all know, whose wealth counts to them for as much as high lineage and a title. They go to court, they are invited to all the grand entertainments of the nobility, and for no reason in the world except that they are millionaires. They are good people enough, charitable people enough, but no more virtuous, no more charitable than you or I, whom the court and the nobility would never think of placing on an equality with themselves. This worship of wealth with virtue combined, merely for its own sake, may be some excuse for the worship of wealth tainted with vice; but it is not much. In both cases the virtue and the vice are the elements least considered.

The love of a lord is another example of candle-holding. There is no lord so disreputable that he will not find respectable middle-class folks who will be proud of his acquaintance. We all have some knowledge of disreputable lords. There are always two or three of them floating about in middle-class society. They may be said to be poor devils, who, being cast out from the grand world, find some consolation in the worship of the little world below. They are lords who have been " dismissed the service," who have disgraced themselves in betting transactions, who have been sent to prison for assaulting the police, who have figured in actions for crim. con.; lords with very dirty hands indeed. But let their hands be never so dirty, there are always plenty of respectable middle-class people eager to grasp them, and proud of the honour of being noticed by a lord.

Yonder goes my Lord Tom Noddy, of crim. con. notoriety, with little Timkins's wife. Little Timkins walks behind, proud to tell everybody that the lady on his lordship's arm is Mrs. Timkins. Mr. and Mrs. Timkins accept invitations to meet his lordship at Miss Demirep's balls and parties, which, it is well known, are paid for by his lordship. Mrs. Timkins thinks Miss Demirep a most agreeable person.

Yonder, in a private box, sits Snobson with Lord Dicebox, dismissed from the service for cheating at play. Snobson sits well forward, that people may see he is in good company.

It may be said that these are gross and extreme cases, and that the persons who toady notoriously bad characters because they are rich or have handles to their names are not fair representatives of respectable society. Let us, then, probe a little deeper, and see if the best of us are not in other ways equally guilty of the meanness and hypocrisy of holding the candle. The motives of the toady are not always sordid: he bows down to other things besides wealth and rank.

There are some of us who worship genius, who habitually permit the great ability of a man to blind us to glaring defects in his moral character.

In every social relation he may be a bad man; but he is a famous poet, or painter, or sculptor, or actor; and we are proud to know him and shake hands with him. We do even worse than this: we countenance vulgar notoriety. A certain person, by some audacity, some preëminency in shamelessness, becomes the talk of the town. It is well known that this person is a vile character; yet he or she soon becomes a subject of half-admiring conversation in our family circles. We are curious to hear about them, we turn in the street to look at them, their names become household words in the mouths of our innocent children. It makes one blush for human nature to think how good men and good women have abased themselves before the vilest of mankind. The days are not yet past when pious clergymen hold the candle to Jezebel in the hope of a good word (towards preferment) from painted lips. The ink is scarcely dry on the page of history which records how a pious queen so far forgot her character and her position as to write a letter of thanks to a dishonoured and abandoned woman who helped her to a shameful legacy.

In many seemingly little but really important matters the best of us are constantly holding the candle to the devil. Let us look nearer home. There is a neighbour of ours, one of our own class, in the same condition of life as ourselves.

He is a very bad man — a bad husband, a bad father, bad in every domestic relation. We know this, and yet we keep up an acquaintance with him, visit him, ask him to our house, and never venture to reproach him with his conduct; though the moment he leaves our door-step we throw up our hands, turn up our eyes, and exclaim, " What a cruel, wicked, bad man!" We hold our best wax-candles to this devil; when, if we were but commonly honest, we should shut our doors in his face.

Then, again, there is the man whose sole recommendation is his power to amuse us with quaint stories and witty sayings. He is a very bad character indeed—positively dishonest, it may be — but yet we tolerate and countenance him because he is an amusing dog. If he were not amusing, we should regard his presence as a contamination.

Gentlemen, worthy of the name in other respects, are too much in the habit of leading one life at home and another out of doors. They pass with the greatest ease from the pure thoughts, pure conversation, and gentle behaviour of the domestic circle, to the ribald talk and licentious manners of the club smoking-room.

Even the parson relaxes when he comes down from the pulpit, and will not scruple to talk lightly of the sins and follies of mankind. Who has not known a clergyman laugh at a queer story told over the wine at some hospitable board? It is not that he is afraid, from motives of interest, to rebuke the impropriety, but that, in deference to the easy habit of society, he permits himself to be too complaisant.

Other examples of candle-holding, of various shades and degrees of criminality, will occur to everyone who is accustomed to study the actions and motives of mankind; and I am afraid that the conclusion which we must all arrive at is, that the whole fabric of society is cemented with hypocrisy, and plastered over, so to speak, with a thin compo' of insincere politeness. It is a difficult thing to keep a pure heart in this worldly world. Robert Burns sorely felt this when he wrote to his friend Mr. Hill: "I am out of all patience with this vile world for one thing. Mankind are by nature benevolent creatures, except in a few scoundrelly instances. I do not think that avarice of the good things we chance to have is born with us; but we are placed here amid so much poverty and want that we are under a cursed necessity of studying selfishness in order that we may exist."

Yes, we may pity the poor who are vicious from necessity, but we should have no toleration for the rich who sin out of mere politeness and the desire to please.

Some earthy philosopher has said, that if every

person were on all occasions to speak his mind and say exactly what he thinks, the world would be intolerable. It is very convenient to believe that; but is it true? Would not the world be far more tolerable if honest true-hearted men and women would resolutely refuse to countenance every kind of hypocrisy, and suffer no kind of custom or politeness which is not founded upon sincerity? If society would band itself together for this object, the sheep would be separated from the goats, and honest folks would know their friends from their foes. It cannot be said that any man is a gentleman who permits himself to associate with, or tolerate, persons who are not gentlemen, or that anyone is pure who holds fellowship with the impure.

ADAPTING FROM THE FRENCH.

By JOHN HOLLINGSHEAD.

BOW STREET.

MR. MORTON SCHNEIDER, who had been out on bail, and who described himself as an English dramatic author, was brought up on remand, charged with stealing a pocket-handkerchief from the person of M. Adolphe Hyacinthe, a French "man of letters," residing at the Hôtel de Provence, Leicester-square, London. The prosecution was conducted by Mr. Coke, from the office of Coke and Littleton, and the prisoner was defended by Mr. Shadrach, of the firm of Shadrach and Abednego. The prosecutor, who was examined through M. Albert, the sworn interpreter of the court, deposed that he was walking through Leicester-square, his custom always of an afternoon, on Thursday the 18th of October, when he felt a slight tug at the tails of his coat, and turning rapidly round with great quickness, he observed the prisoner walking quickly with great rapidity up a side street, court, or alley, leading into Soho, with what appeared to be his (the prisoner's) handkerchief in his hands. He (the prosecutor) followed him (the prisoner); but was unable to catch him, owing to his (the prosecutor's) ignorance of the sinuous tortuosities of the neighbourhood. He saw no more of the prisoner for several days, until he met him promiscuously by chance at a *table d'hôte* or ordinary, held at a house near the Haymarket, much frequented or " used" by literary men. The prisoner then had the same handkerchief, which he openly displayed, as if rather proud of it, and the prosecutor noticed that the prisoner had had his, the rightful owner's, name taken out of the corner of the said handkerchief, and his own name put in its place.

Cross-examined by Mr. Shadrach.

Was not the handkerchief thoroughly cleaned when you last saw it?

Prosecutor. It was.

Mr. Shadrach. Was it not very dirty — very unfit for an English audience — I mean an Englishman — when you say you last had it in your possession?

Prosecutor. I cannot say.

Mr. Shadrach. Don't beat about the bush, sir; tell the court the whole truth and nothing but the truth; was it not filthy dirty when you lost it, and clean and irreproachable when you found it?

The learned magistrate here interposed.

Do you admit the possession of the handkerchief, Mr. Shadrach?

Mr. Shadrach. We do, your worship, and shall soon show our defence when we have finished the cross-examination of the prosecutor.

The cross-examination then continued.

Mr. Shadrach (to the prosecutor). You have not answered my last question; was not the handkerchief spotless when you last saw it?

The prosecutor, after consulting for a few moments with his solicitor, Mr. Coke, admitted that it had been cleaned.

Mr. Shadrach. And a new name put in the corner of it?

Prosecutor. Certainly.

Mr. Coke having declined to ask any questions, Mr. Shadrach addressed the learned magistrate for the defence. He contended, on the part of the prisoner, Mr. Morton Schneider, that the appropriation of this handkerchief did not amount to stealing within the meaning of the Act; it was simply a bold and successful adaptation from the French. The word "steal" was an ugly word, too often used in connection with transactions in which annexation, or less offensive terms, would be more appropriate. The prisoner, Mr. Morton

Schneider, was a well-known literary man, and a member of the Dramatic Authors' Society. In the exercise of his vocation he had often taken pieces—that is, little dramas—and other property from the French, and amongst the rest from the prosecutor, M. Adolphe Hyacinthe. The prosecutor had never complained, or, if he had complained, had never brought his complaint before a legal tribunal. He allowed himself to be stripped of literary property worth many pounds sterling without saying a word, but made all the present fuss about a paltry handkerchief of the value of a few shillings. Mr. Morton Schneider never adopted more than one course in dealing with French property. What he did to French plays he did to French pocket-handkerchiefs. He relieved them, if he might be allowed the term, of all offensive impurities, made them English in fact, and acceptable to the fastidious British public, and was justly entitled to put his own name or initials in the place of the name or initials of the coarser Frenchman, author and proprietor. Adaptation like this, he contended, was an art, and not a crime. Even admitting, which he, Mr. Shadrach, was not at all prepared to admit, that in adaptation the line ought to be drawn at pocket-handkerchiefs, still Mr. Morton Schneider ought not to suffer for an offence which the law had neglected to define. He should ask the learned magistrate to dismiss the case.

Mr. Coke made no remark, and the learned magistrate took time to consider his decision. The court was crowded with adapters, and there was an attempt at applause near the close of Mr. Shadrach's speech, but it was quickly suppressed.

My Ultimatum.

I.

Who talks to me of " giving up "—
    Of lying down despairing?
Who says the bitter in his cup
    Is bitter past the bearing?
For *me*, I feel the thing to do
    (Let fate be hard or tender)
Is—like *La Garde* at Waterloo—
    To die and not surrender.

II.

What fierce encounters I have had,
    Escapes how very narrow!
My first affray was with a lad
    Who bore a bow and arrow.
If I should ever fight again
    That old and young offender,
I see my course before me plain—
    To die and not surrender.

III.

And then I ran a race to snatch
    A laurel from Apollo,
Whom very few contrive to catch,
    And very many follow.
Amidst the throng of sons of song,
    The bards of either gender—
E'en yet I pant and limp along—
    To die and not surrender.

IV.

I strove with Plutus day and night,
    But left the fray in dudgeon;
And now I wage a fiercer fight
    With Tempus, old curmudgeon.
Go on, Destroyer!—*you* destroy,
    And Art shall be the mender.
Gray hair?—I'll get a wig, my boy,
    Or *dye* and not surrender!

HENRY S. LEIGH.

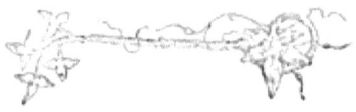

"Begotten of Sad Stars."

By the Author of "The Waterdale Neighbours."

A FRENCHMAN of genius has devoted some bitter and thrilling words to a description of what he calls "the odious race of the unappreciated." The phrase is sharp and cynical; but there is only too much truth under its sarcasm. He died himself, poor fellow, in a hospital, and his name is a scandal and a shuddering to the successful, the appreciated, and above all the virtuous. But in good truth they are an odious race, the unappreciated. They have generally much more self-conceit than the successful—just as ugly women commonly have a far higher opinion of themselves than handsome women—and they are all egotism and grievance, and they are cruel, relentless bores. Of course, even the unappreciated have their merits, and some of them are positively heroic in their fierce futile combats with the wind of public opinion which blows over them unheeding; and others are more heroic still in the dignity with which they accept their fate. It is a grand endowment, the faculty of knowing how to fail; and the unappreciated sometimes, not often, possess it. But to appreciate the unappreciated, you must not see them too often or too near. It has been my lot to see a good many of them, and very closely, and I have a short story to tell of one who was a bore indeed, but went very, very near to being a lion; and who had to succumb at last, to clip Elysium and resign his chances of fame, not because of any fault or deficiency of his own, but only because fate and the world, and the flesh of officialism, and the devil of delay, were too strong for him, and crushed him.

Perhaps of all unfortunate and pitiable race of men under the sun of English civilisation the most unfortunate and pitiable are the race of inventors and discoverers. *Sic vos non vobis* is their motto and their epitaph—that is, when their discovery is real, when their invention is worth anything. A miserable personage was the poet of Grub-street and the Dunciad. A sad poor dog was the broken-down Bohemian of the Quartier Latin in the old days, when there was a

Bohemia, and when the Garden of the Luxembourg was yet unmenaced by the Prefect of the Seine. An Irish poor scholar, tramping the country with shoeless feet and empty stomach, was not an exhilarating spectacle. But the worst of these forlorn ones was happy compared with the brokendown, luckless, unsuccessful inventor. The Grubstreet hacks had their hours of cheap revelry, the Bohemian had his snatches of delirious joy, when they forgot booksellers and creditors, the grinding of verses and the invention of plots. But your scientific inventor has no reprieve. Science is a remorseless mistress. She never leaves your poor tortured brain when once you have allowed her to take exclusive possession of it. She is with you always, suggesting dreadful new combinations, racking you with fresh calculations, putting you through fearful mental processes as you eat your bread, steeping crucial problems which will not dissolve in your cup, stuffing your sleepless pillow with angles, and wheels, and decimals, and fossils, and salts, and parallaxes, and other such torments of the weary brain.

As editor of a journal in a great busy shipbuilding, manufacturing, stock-broking town, I had many painful opportunities at one time of knowing the unsuccessful inventor or discoverer. Sometimes he came in the full flush and bouncing buoyancy of first discovery, and seemed to offer

quite as a favour to a journalist the chance of
learning something in advance about the grand
project which was to awaken the world. The new
paddle or screw which was to cross the Atlantic
in three days; the mechanical contrivance which
was to supersede steam; the explosive material to
do away with gunpowder; the never-failing fire-
extinguisher; the balloon capable of being guided
anywhere; the telescope destined to resolve the
most distant nebulæ; the new method of printing;
the universal-language scheme; the one only true
and new theory of currency;—how often, O, how
often, have such projects been expounded to my
exhausted ears! The new and fresh inventor is
hopeful and triumphant. He is very familiar
with the names of Ministers of State, great scientific men, and mighty steamship builders and contractors; and they are all positively fascinated
with his scheme. "I explained it all to Stanley,
sir, myself, and he was quite taken with it; and
Stanley has promised me to bring it at once under
the notice of the Cabinet." "Brassey saw it in
a moment; I think he is prepared to make any
terms with me." "Brewster admitted my prin-
ciple at once." "You should have seen how
Herschell caught at the idea." This is well
enough; but the poor broken-down creature,
whose invention or discovery dates from years
back, and who has been vainly knocking at every

door, and buttonholing every influential man ever since, is only a sad spectacle. His cheeks are hollow, his chin is badly shorn, his eyes have a ghostly light in them, his hands tremble with eagerness and weakness together—there is not a gleam of shirt anywhere visible about him. He can only tell you mournfully of his genius, his grand discovery, and his disappointment. Sometimes he borrows half-a-crown, but not often. I do not know why it is, but I have found that though science makes paupers as well as literature, she has not the same faculty of making beggars. Sometimes the unappreciated inventor presents himself in more stormy fashion, with fierce tale of personal grievances, affecting every Minister or living ex-Minister, with bundles of correspondence tending to prove corruption, malice, hatred, nay, high treason on the part of at least three successive Presidents of the Board of Trade or First Lords of the Admiralty or War Secretaries. He expects you to read his papers, and take up his quarrel, and write leading articles calling for the instant impeachment of the traitor, of all the traitors: and if you do take his papers and read them, and find, as you knew you must find, that he has not a ghost of a case against anybody, he persecutes you for days and weeks, insisting upon convincing you; and, failing in that, goes away at last, and adds you to the list of his purchased and perjured enemies. One can put up with him, however. But when the inventor is a manly, patient, dignified being, in whose clear sad eye you read genuine intellect and devotion unappreciated,—one who your instinct tells you is surely in the right, and yet who, your experience of the world convinces you, will never make either money or fame by his invention; it is hard to think him a bore, even when most he bores you —it is impossible not to wonder at the malign fate which condemns genius and perseverance and patience to no better business than the wasting out of a life in the pursuit of something which, even if found and brought to full light, will only at best make another fortune for a capitalist, and hardly win a spray of laurel to throw upon the finder's grave.

The man I have especially to speak of now was a discoverer, not an inventor. His name was Hamilton Seamark, and he made my acquaintance rather abruptly.

In the provinces, a newspaper editor is not an impersonal creature, an influence, an unseen Jove hidden away in Olympian clouds, and heard only in his thunders. He is known of all men, and his editorial room is as often as not a sort of *salon*, club, or council-chamber for the little notabilities of the place. Therefore, Mr. Seamark, whom I had never seen before, had no difficulty in making his way into my room one evening. He had a bundle of papers with him, but I did not at first see in him an inventor or discoverer. He was more like an artist, or the conventional type of poet which still is to be found in some parts of the provinces. He was young, very young, small, slight and handsome, with worn cheeks and bright restless eyes. When he began to talk, he talked with amazing rapidity and much accompaniment of energetic gesture. After a little, I found that he had a cough which might have satisfied the notions of artistic propriety avowed by Feuillet's Delilah.

"I want you to get me justice," he said, after some very rapid preliminaries of self-introduction. "Justice. You can get it: they will listen to you; they only listen to newspaper fellows now; a man of science, a man of genius is worse than nothing. I am a man of science."

"And a man of genius, doubtless," I added.

That was my sneer, you see; for I was offended by his manner of alluding to the British press, the palladium of &c. &c.

"And a man of genius," he quickly replied. "I have arrived at a discovery by the sheer force of genius that their hirelings never could have lighted on with all their instruments and their labour."

"Their hirelings," I continued—still sarcastic

—"are, I presume, the hirelings of the British Government?"

"They are."

"Board of Trade, or Admiralty, or War Office, perhaps?"

"None of these. I am an astronomer."

"O!" This was quite out of my line.

He laid a bundle of papers on my table, went to the doors—there were two in the room—looked cautiously out, to make sure that no one was within hearing, then closed the doors, came up to my desk, and gazing into my eyes with eyes that gleamed, he said: "I have discovered a new planet!"

I was on the point of replying, like the hero in the play of *The Irish Ambassador* when solemnly and secretly informed by a mysterious diplomatist that he "has seen the Swedish Ambassador"—"The devil you have!" The announcement appeared to me so very uninteresting that I could not understand why my new acquaintance should be at all excited about it.

He saw by my face that I did not care much about the discovery.

"Don't you know what a planet is?" he asked sharply and querulously. "Look here; I'll explain."

"Thank you; you really need not explain to me what a planet is. You say you have discovered a new one."

"I *have* discovered a new one. Good heavens! do you think such a thing can be a matter of opinion? It is a matter of fact."

"Very well; you have discovered a new planet. What can I do in the matter?"

Then came the explanation, in an exposition so long that I should certainly have fallen asleep but for the vivacity, the energy, the bitter complaints, the querulous, feverish impatience with which it was ornamented. At times the earnestness of my lecturer rose to a passion that had something in it sublime; at times his manner was like that of a disappointed schoolgirl, who only waits to get out of the room in order to burst fairly into tears. I was somewhat surprised. A poet, whose first work had just been birched by the *Saturday Review*, might have gone on in such a strain; but a scientific man, a student of the stars, who claimed to have found a new planet!

I became interested, however; and I, at last, got to understand his story. I spare the reader technical details, which then bewildered me, and would bewilder me again if I were to attempt to explain them. Enough to say, that for years this youth—he was about five-and-twenty—had been absorbed in an effort to account for the perturbations of a certain planet, and had become convinced that they were caused by the existence of another planet hitherto unknown. Without a great telescope, without access to any observatory, without any assistance worth speaking of from the calculations of eminent astronomers, he had gradually constructed a perfect scheme of the place, orbit, and motions of the unknown planet: he had found it, in fact, only he had not seen it. No telescope he could get at was of any use for the purpose: perhaps none yet made could find it. But there it was. Every test that science could help him to apply, short of that final test, he had applied, and the result had been to make his discovery a certainty. Yet he had dunned our official department of astronomy in letter after letter in vain. He asked that the great observatories might be set to work to find his planet with telescopes—to test his calculations, to acknowledge his discovery — in vain. They would not go into the question. He received polite and chilling answers, the most decisive being to the effect that no man could make such calculations—as he *had* made. He was in other words quietly told that he was an amateur, a sciolist, a dreamer; a man who had made a wild guess, and then invented calculations to support it.

This I learned during our first interview. I knew, of course, just as much about astronomy as most journalists and literary men do—that is to say, almost nothing. But I understood his case, and I thought he had been treated with unfair neglect, and I was anxious to do my best to serve him. What could I do? Little or nothing. We might, of course, have made public his supposed discovery and his calculations. This I was anxious to do; but Seamark shrank from publishing a word until he had obtained positive conviction and proof of his discovery. "I have not found the planet—actually found it," he said. "To publish my conviction and my calculations will be only to enable some other to make the final discovery, and claim share of the honour."

All I could do, then, was to write letters and back up his appeals; and I need not tell the readers of these papers how supreme is a provincial journalist's influence over the official lords of State science.

But Seamark and I became friends. He was a terrible bore sometimes; and I often told him so. He had only his one subject. He sometimes dined with me and a few other friends; and he was silent as an owl, until we were left alone, or were walking home together: and then *itur ad astra* again.

One night we were thus going home: Seamark was unusually reticent. Several times he began to say something confusedly, as if he had a confidence to make of which he felt half-ashamed. At last I said:

"Come, Seamark, you have something to tell

me—out with it. Anything wrong in the calculations?"

"Wrong in the calculations! Stuff! What ignorant men you journalists are! Do you think mathematics and numbers change like the fashions?"

"Wish they did. There would be variety."

"But I have something to tell you. Only I am really ashamed—you will think me such an idiot."

"Perhaps. But tell me all the same."

"Then—to come to the point—" He stood still, and looked down. "I am haunted. I see a perpetual spectre at my side."

"Haunted! The haunted man! Come, this is too much—a savant and a Positivist sees a ghost, and believes in it!"

Seamark, I should say, was an indomitable Positivist.

"I don't say I believe in it; but I see it. Listen to me. Always when I shut my eyes—often while they are open and in broad day—now, at this moment, while I look at that pavement, I see my ghost!"

"And what form does the grisly phantom wear?"

"The worst he could assume in my eyes. I see—" and Seamark smiled a wan and dreary smile—"I see a man who is at work with a star-map and a telescope, and is trying to find out my planet. I have seen him this long time. I can mark his progress. He started much later than I did; but he has maps and instruments I cannot get, and he is on the verge of success. Mark my words, he will complete his task before I do, and he will have the fame, and I shall die unknown."

The thing was past laughing at. The deep genuine despair and agony in the face of the poor young fellow were cruel to look at.

"I don't wonder at all," I said as cheerily as I could, "that you should have visions of this kind. A man who works and thinks at least eighteen hours out of the twenty-four, who drinks little and eats less, must have phantoms of some kind; and one can easily trace the genesis of your goblin. The feverish child sees mad bulls coming to gore him: the mad bull you fear is a rival astronomer. There is your ghost for you! A little rest and change of air would lay him soon enough. I wish, Seamark, you would fall in love."

"You must not think," he said irresolutely—disregarding my last suggestion—"that I believe in any silly rubbish about spectral visitations. But we know very little of the more occult laws of the universe. There may be secret influences and forces, and—"

"Yes; I have heard all that before. I think

the Davenport Brothers used to appeal to the possible existence of such laws to explain their tomfoolery. But they were not scientific men, or Positivists."

"At all events," he said, "this thing I see is not subjective. How could it be? I tell you I see this man's face now as plainly as I see yours. I could make his portrait if I were a painter."

"I saw a face last night in a dream as plainly as ever I saw a real face in my life."

"Ah, but you don't see the same face always." He sighed wearily, and we said no more on the subject. Nor did I speak to him of it when we next met.

A few days after, I called to see him, and found him looking more depressed than ever. He said, with a ghastly twitching of the face, something between a spasm and a smile:

"My rival makes terrible progress. He will distance me yet."

I made up my mind that day to speak to a physician, a personal friend of mine and a man of vigorous intelligence, free from any of the pedantry of his profession, about the condition of my poor young astronomer. Meantime I insisted on dragging Seamark out for a walk. Usually when we thus went out we sought green fields, quiet roads, and solitude. Now I thought the sight of a bustling street would be far more enlivening and distracting. So we walked down the principal street of the town. The day was bright, frosty, cheery, in late December. The street was crowded, noisy, busy as Regent-street. Carriages were at every shop-door. There were glimpses everywhere of feathers and velvets and furs, of pretty faces, bright petticoats, symmetrical ankles. I insisted on Seamark's looking at everything and everybody. Some photographs in a window attracted me. I dragged him to the shop to look at them.

He was about to turn carelessly away when something caught his eye, and his whole face flushed up. He seized me by the arm, and said in a loud and eager tone, to the amazement of some idlers who, like ourselves, were looking at the photographs:

"Look there! Look at that face! That is my rival! That is the man who is destined to forestall me!"

I looked at the photograph he pointed to. It stood in a row with Mr. Gladstone, the Bishop of Oxford, Miss Menken, Professor Owen, and, I think, Leotard. It bore no name. It was the face of a thin, intellectual man, with bald forehead and square jaw.

"That is he," said Seamark, now more calm; "that is the face I always see. It is an excellent photograph; for I see the real face this very moment."

I began to think the bystanders would regard my friend as a madman; I therefore gladly assented to his proposal that we should go in and buy the photograph. How I longed that it might prove to be the likeness of some eminent Chancery lawyer or agricultural member of Parliament!

The young woman in the shop, when asked who the photograph represented, took it out of the case, looked at the back of it, and found the name written in pencil. She boggled rather over the reading of it. "It was a foreign name," she said.

Seamark seized the *carte* rather abruptly and read out the name. It was that of a great living French astronomer.

"You see!" he said to me with a glance half-triumphant, half-sad.

He paid for the photograph and we came away.

"I see," said I, when we were in the street, "the solution now of the whole mystery. No doubt you had seen the portrait of the great astronomer before, and it stamped itself on your memory; and in your anxiety about your discovery his face arose in your mind as that of one likely to be a rival. The whole thing is obvious."

"I never in my life saw a portrait of that man before."

"You may have seen it and forgotten it, yet the impression—"

"I tell you I could not have forgotten it. I never saw his portrait before. I was reading one of his lectures only last night, and it never even occurred to me that he could be the man. Do you think I could have failed, then, to remember his face if I had ever seen it?"

I argued no more, for he was becoming painfully excited. Undoubtedly the thing was strange; but I felt convinced then—indeed, I am inclined to think still—that my explanation, or something very like it, was the true solution of the apparent mystery. But the impression wrought on the excitable and overtasked mind of poor Seamark was profound. I suggested that he should communicate with the French astronomer, who was a man of noble reputation, and especially remarkable for his sympathetic kindness to young *savants*. But Seamark would hear of nothing of the kind. "Alone," he replied, "or not at all,—all, or nothing."

I confess I began to doubt whether there was really anything in my friend's discovery. It seemed impossible to suppose that our Astronomer Royal could be indifferent to his urgencies if they really merited serious attention. Seamark afterwards told me that he had received a series of questions or tests from the Observatory, designed, I understood, to prove rather the extent of his capacity to make a discovery, than the probabilities of the discovery itself; and that he had treated them with disdain—refused, in fact, to take any notice of them. It need hardly be said how little he served his object by such a proceeding.

A few nights after, I returned late to my lodgings. I was a bachelor, and had furnished apartments, first-floor front, in a house which stood in a long, gaunt, broad, monotonous street, ending in a great square, on which my windows gave a side-glance. I had been writing a good deal all day, and was tired, but not sleepy; and the sky over the broad moonlit square attracted me much, and led me to fall into a dreamy way of thinking about poor Seamark and his fatal discovery, and his spectral second-sight. The stars had a personal interest for me now, which I may confess they never had before. And yet my intimacy with Seamark had to a great extent robbed them of their poetry, and converted them into pitiless mathematical taskmasters, whom their votaries celebrate in numbers that are only arithmetical. Nothing could be more hard, mechanical, prosaic than the life which poor Seamark led, devoted to his evil stars. The only poetic attribute of this star-worship was its cruelty. Messalina expected less of her adorers than did Seamark's ruthless invisible mistress, the accursed unknown planet-Isis, which he was doomed to adore.

Suddenly I saw a figure, dark against the moonlight, come hurrying across the square. I knew the slight boyish form. It was a keenly cold night, but poor Seamark wore no overcoat. He came striding along to the house where I lived, looked up at the window, and seeing no light (I had refrained from lighting my gas that I might not spoil my star-gazing) he hesitated, then stamped vehemently and seemed about to hurry away. I opened the window and called to him.

"Let me in," he said; "I want to speak to you. I have bad, bad news."

I hurried down and opened the door: we came upstairs. Before telling me anything he pointed to a decanter that stood on a side-table.

"Is that brandy?" he asked eagerly.

"It is." I was surprised at the question. He poured out a glassful and drank it—he who was usually a hater of all stimulants.

"Now, Seamark, what is your bad news,— nothing dreadfully bad, I hope?"

"Only that it's all over," he said. "There's an end to all my hopes and my labours. I am late. He has found it!"

I knew quite well what he meant, and I assumed, of course, that some public announcement had claimed for the French astronomer the honour of the discovery.

"Are you sure?" I asked. "Have you read anything about it yourself—with your own eyes?"

"Read with my own eyes!" he exclaimed in bitter tones; "I saw with my own eyes. I saw him in his observatory—I saw him point the telescope, I saw his look of final triumph. I saw him note down the spot—the hour—minutes and seconds. It is all over. I have thrown away these years—for nothing!"

"Then you only saw this in your dream, or vision, or whatever it is?"

"Nothing on earth can be more certain than what I saw. I knew this long time back—I knew it must come to this; and yet I feel as if I must go mad."

And indeed he talked and raved for a while like one going mad. He stormed and cursed at Astronomers Royal, and scientific authorities, and the world, and fate, and himself. At last he sat on the sofa, pressed his thin white hands to his face, and fairly burst into a passion of tears. As I looked at him, my eyes fixed only on his forehead, his long loose hair, his fair delicate fingers through which the tear-drops came streaming, I might have thought I gazed at the passionate anguish of a forsaken girl. Then it struck me for the first time how singularly girlish were his form, his face, his gestures—his nature. Never before or since have I known such a human paradox. That penetrating, far-reaching, indomitable intellect, which had grappled alone and unassisted with calculations so abstruse and difficult that they seemed beyond the stretch of man's unaided brain,—how came it to be cooped up in that frail feminine body along with that fitful, passionate, weak, feminine nature? As the unhappy young man sat there and sobbed, one felt almost compelled to take his hand and soothe and pet him, so wonderfully did he resemble a weeping woman.

Seamark remained with me that night. We sat up nearly all night, and I have to confess that I made him drink a good deal of brandy. He calmed and brightened of course, just as a girl does, after his outburst of tears, but his conviction of the reality of what he had seen was unshaken.

Did I believe in it? I affected not to; but in my heart I think I had now become almost as credulous as he. Yet I started as if I too had seen something preternatural when, on opening *Galignani* a few days after, just as the post had brought it, I read a lengthened account of the discovery of a new planet made at the Paris Observatory by poor Seamark's rival. It was Seamark's planet.

Of course we then wrote and published, and vindicated his claims—too late. The French astronomer behaved most generously, and frankly declared on examination of the whole question that he was convinced Seamark was really the first discoverer. Our official astronomers expressed a polite regret that Seamark had not furnished the calculations they sought, which might, they thought, perhaps have led to a decisive discovery prior to that of the Frenchman—to whom now, of course, they felt bound to award the honour. Seamark's name bubbled for a little while on the surface of scientific controversy, and then disappeared. The French astronomer is accepted by the world and by science as the discoverer of the planet.

Seamark ought, perhaps, to have dramatically died or killed himself then; but he lived, and after a while got over his cruel disappointment, and went to work afresh among his pitiless stars. I removed to London, and for a while lost sight of him; but I heard of him for the last time some year or two back. He joined a scientific party which set out to make astronomical observations in the Southern Seas; in a night of storm he was washed off the deck of the vessel in mid-ocean and drowned. By a freak of fate, which seems almost as strange as the one inexplicable part of the story I have told, he was doomed to lie in death where the stars to which he gave up his life could not even shine upon his grave.

THE RAVEN.

From the German.

By John Oxenford.

I.

The moon is bright, and clear the sky;
    The robber from the gibbet swings;
The Raven from the wood must hie,
    For mighty hunger stirs his wings.

II.

He scents the dainty feast afar,
    And first of all the guests will be;
And widely spread his pinions are,
    As loud he croaks—"The best for me!"

III.

He picks the carcass at his ease,
    Until the face arrests his gaze,
When suddenly his cawings cease—
    What can the Raven thus amaze?

IV.

It is his master—sure enough—
　　The man who kept him long ago,
And often from his hand so rough
　　A sav'ry morsel would bestow:

V.

He gave him meat, he gave him bread,
　　He call'd him " Bonny Jack," of old;
Now hangs he on the gibbet dead;
　　The kindly hand is stiff and cold:

VI.

He patted him in days long past,
　　And smiled on him with kindly eyes:—
The bird has found his lord at last,
　　And shrieking from the gibbet flies.

VII.

He hears the croakings loud and glad
　　Of other ravens by his side:
Poor Jack, they think, is surely mad—
　　The taste of flesh he can't abide.

VIII.

The moon is bright, the sky is clear,
　　The robber from the gibbet swings;
One bird, to whom his lord was dear,
　　His way into the forest wings!

Terrible Telegrams.

BY THOMAS ARCHER.

I AM of opinion that some place of residence should be provided for quiet old-fashioned people who find it impossible to accustom themselves to the rapid and to them most obnoxious changes (misnamed "improvements") which are supposed to be essential to what is called progress. Such people as myself, for instance, who cannot run, and are equally unable to get out of the way, are continually being knocked down by the wheels of the triumphal car of the nineteenth century. Cannot the Government set apart a suburb for our especial benefit;—a place to which no local railway has yet penetrated; where no hansom cabs linger along the roadways for the purpose of making furious dashes at timid pedestrians who venture on a crossing; where clean and genteel flys may be hired of a civil

John Palmer, del.   Dalziel Bros., sc.

THE TELEGRAM.

stable-keeper; and a couple of sedan chairs, retained for ordinary evening visitations in the next street, to be carried by the carpet-beater and general odd-man and messenger, assisted by the son of the small-coal man or the greengrocer? It may be replied that there are suburbs already in existence, where such a condition of things might easily be inaugurated,—suburbs, or, at all events, adjacent though outlying country places, where there are as yet no railway stations. I can only say, I don't know one in which, directly a few select inhabitants take quiet possession in the hope of remaining undisturbed by the restless, soulless, mechanical activity of the age, a speculative builder does not run up hideous streets of semi-detached villas, and form a colony of stockbrokers' clerks and aspiring tradespeople, who leave their shops behind daily at five o'clock. The consequence is, that to take these people to town every morning there is an omnibus competition which entirely excludes the original residents from all the inside seats; and finally, a branch railway, and a wretched, horribly new stone-and-stucco station disfigures the place; the best walks are cut up and spoilt; the streets are infested with hordes of navigators, who demoralise the labouring population and increase the number of the beershops, and we are all scared by day and kept sleepless by night by the scream and rattle of the trains. The whole scandalous proceeding is consummated by the arrival of a telegraphic apparatus and the newspapers; nasty closely-printed unwieldy great broadsheets, from which if anybody ventures to read them—and it is what I never could bring my mind to do—the ink all comes off upon one's gloves and soils one's muslin dress. It is to the telegrams that I personally have the greatest aversion, however: not that there is any objection whatever to the curious discovery of the powers of electricity. The wonders of science as exhibited at the Polytechnic, where I make a point of going twice a year, have ever been a source of gratification to me; and I would have them made useful in the instruction of youth at half price; but nothing now is too high or too sacred for trade; or, as those who are ashamed to call it by its right name, say, "for the advancement of commercial interests." Of all the modern inventions which have served to overthrow sentiment among us, to abolish refinement, and to use the results of a high material civilisation for the purpose of establishing a mental and spiritual barbarism, I regard the Electric Telegraph as the worst. Telegrams (the very word is, I am told, a barbarous and illiterate jargon) are illustrative of what is called modern progress— of the progress which leaves everything best worth having behind, and, for the sake of living faster, enjoys nothing. If they have not almost abolished writing, they have at least nearly put an end to epistolary correspondence. We get no letters now; only brief uninteresting and frequently ungrammatical communications, scrawled illegibly on a tiny scrap of flimsy tissue note-paper. Who ever receives a good, honest, earnest letter now-a-days? —a letter which the writer has sat down to as to a labour of love, and, warming with the task, has extended over a fair sheet of gilt-edged post, *and then crossed?* In a few more years there will be nobody left who keeps packets of letters tied up with ribbon, in secret nooks and drawers of their desks and bureaus. There will be no desks and bureaus, perhaps; no letters certainly; it will all be done by telegram, and an invitation will be sent an hour before dinner-time, with just "4.30 sharp" upon it; and the reply will be, "Yes, thanks." This, however, is sarcasm. It ill becomes me to satirise that which should rather be regarded with serious grief; for consider how much letters have had to do with the lives of people like myself: how almost every epoch in our quiet existences has been marked by epistolary correspondence. I never received but two of those dreadful telegrams in my life, and one of them was delivered to me in mistake for somebody else. It contained only these words:

"All right. A girl. Both doing well."

It gave me a dreadful shock, for I remembered how the advent of a little stranger in our family had always been accompanied by a series of observances which indicated that an immortal being had been ushered into the world. There was first a white kid glove on the knocker, then a cushion stuck with pins of welcome, next the solemn whispering reception of visitors by the young mother, who sat up in a lace cap and a large white shawl; and of half-crowns by the nurse, who assiduously produced light refreshments on the occasion; then there was the christening, with white favours and a quiet party; and a silver mug, a papboat, a coral and bells from godfathers and godmothers. All these ceremonies were the occasion of letters which kept alive family affection, and made life something more than a mere passing reminder, and time worth a better record than the mere memorandum of a railway clerk.

Letters were a part of the observances of society in those days. There were proper seasons and occasions for them, quite independent of anything happening which required to be communicated—at Christmas-tide especially, and on New-Year's day, and birthdays, and on hearing incidentally of some piece of good fortune or any sorrow which had overtaken a friend. I hope we have not yet reached such a pitch of brutality that we could communicate by telegram on any of these occasions, giving our secret thoughts and tender sympathies to the ear of the clerk, and sending them briefly in a couple of lines. I remember even in my school-days how much letters had to do with our daily life. There were the letters that we got from home with the cake and the parcel of fruit, the new writing-desk and the box of toys. Then there were the holiday letters, written just before breaking-up days, wherein we were supposed to write the sentiments of our hearts by beginning " My dear Parents," and declaring our hope that we should " ever be mindful of the constant love and care" bestowed upon us by our dear friends, and " of the inestimable advantages to be derived from the pursuit of those studies to which we were directed by those to whom the care of our education was intrusted." How well I remember the old formula! I have some of my own letters in my desk now, along with those others—those mournful deep-black-bordered ones that came to me with the first great sorrow that almost laid my life low ; but which, coming as messengers of terrible intelligence, had yet something of healing in their wings, because of the love and compassion that dwelt in the words by which that awful message was conveyed. The ink is all brown and faded now, but the remembrance of the sorrow lives, the remembrance of the sorrow and of the tenderness, both of which can be recalled as it were in their first freshness by a glance at those blurred and paling characters.

Shall I, or will anybody who was at school with me, at the Miss Walkintwos' establishment, ever forget the "breaking-up day itself?" This too was anticipated by the receipt of a letter directed to each young lady in the school. We saw the elder Miss Walkintwo write them; we saw the younger Miss Walkintwo (Miss Jane, who took the juniors) seal and direct them; and we knew that when we went up to bed we should find them on our pillows; but they were a part of our proper observance of the proprieties, and we each felt that it gave an air of consummate grace to our breaking-up party to have "the pleasure of our company requested to an evening assembly of the pupils and friends." In the same spirit we all met on the night in question, as though we had not all known for a week before what dresses (down to the minutest end of ribbon) we should each wear. In the same spirit we entered and were received by Mrs. Walkintwo (dear old lady!), in the lace cap which each of the elder girls had been shown separately and secretly in the best bedroom; and by the Misses Walkintwo, who smiled a real welcome to us from their cheery hard-worked anxious-looking faces. Poor ladies! they must have longed for the holiday time even more than we did, though they had their bills to make out and to pay, house to refurbish, and preparations to make for the next half year. In the same spirit we partook of the very thin bread and butter which some of us had seen in the very process of cutting, and of the seed-cake, the odour of which had pervaded the entire house ever since our makeshift dinner at twelve o'clock—and our hurried flight to the mysteries of white muslin toilettes with blue and pink ribbons. Probably the dancing-master and the writing-master had received similar invitations; and even some of the brothers of young ladies (brothers who wore jackets and could dance) were expected to be present.

The dancing-master, Monsieur la Sarre — it was reported by one sarcastic girl that his real name was Lazarus; and he certainly had a very hooky nose, and spoke through it—was resplendent on these occasions in an embroidered velvet waistcoat and a dress-coat lined with white satin, and such small feet, that when he came into the room and bowed, with his hand on his breast, and talked with more of a foreign accent than ever, he looked as though he had been stuck there on two polished ebony wooden legs. Then there was Mr. Ruleight, the drawing- and writing-master, whose daughter was in the school; and once I remember that an old pupil, on her return from her marriage-tour, paid us a visit. Her husband, who called for her in the evening, was a fine man buttoned up to the chin in a tight frock-coat, and with such curly hair and large whiskers that we all thought he was an officer in the army, or at all events a person of great distinction; till that same sarcastic Emma Gogsbury said her brother knew him very well, and that he was a bottled-beer merchant, besides keeping a ham-and-beef shop in the Kingsland-road.

I don't know why I should have grown so garrulous, even though I have lived to be an old maid. Yes, I have none of those other letters in my secretary—letters that tell of the heart's devotion, and of which some of my friends have received so many, and have allowed me to participate in their joy, not always lasting. I might have had, but it was not to be. There came to me one day a black-bordered messenger instead of a white-winged dove, and the page that might have been opened in my book of life was closed for ever. I will not think of that now, not that the thought gives me pain. But I have gone quite away from the subject of telegrams. I said I had only received two. The second was from my dear niece Bertha. She too was educated at the Miss Walkintwos', one of their last pupils previous to their retiring from business; but her parents live in the country, and I have ever tried to act to her as though she had been my own daughter. She is a fiery, imperious creature, for she was a spoilt child always, and very, very beautiful, *I* think. So William thought; for she no sooner left school than he wanted to marry her, and married they were before she was twenty years old. I thought it would have been better for her to have had some household or domestic training first; but that, it appears, has gone out of fashion too. At all events, as her future husband had a good business in the City, they obtained her parents' consent; and my only fear was that her passionate temper might be a trouble to her. Fortunately William was one of the best of men—slow, but with an amiability that nothing could ruffle, and a fine constitution. They were a handsome couple, and I gave them all my old silver tea-service, and the best spoons, for a wedding-present.

They have been married now very little above six months, and I have more than once had occasion to warn Bertha not to give way to her temper, or to try her husband's affection too far. Judge, then, of my surprise, my almost horror, when, the day before yesterday, I received a "telegram" from Bertha, saying no more than—"Dear Aunty, come to me at once; I am so miserable."

You might have knocked me down with a feather; but I sent Hannah for a fly—she brought a cab, and it was full of muddy straw, and somebody had been smoking tobacco inside it—and drove off to Barbarossa-villas at once. What could have happened? When I got in, Bertha flew into my arms and became hysterical.

"What—what is the matter, child?" I exclaimed. "Nothing between you and William, I solemnly hope and trust?"

"I—I was very wicked, and behaved so badly to him this morning; and I deserve it all, and I am a wretch. But O, how could he be so cruel?" she sobbed.

"Why, what has he done?" said I in dismay.

"He went away without a word, or, at all events, I didn't listen, for I went into my own room, and banged the door; but look — look there!"

I saw what it was—a telegram. O, how I loathed the sight of the wretched scrap of blue paper, with its red letters! This was it:

"It is too heavy for me. I cannot come; but it will be brought home to you, and you will have to pay for it."

What was to be done? I tried to cheer her; told her to hope for the best; that he had sent that hateful message in the heat of passion, which would have subsided over the rational employment of writing a letter. It was with difficulty that I could get her to take a cup of tea. Wearily the hours went on—eight, nine, ten, eleven, midnight —and she sat there dumb, weeping, almost heartbroken.

Suddenly there was the sound of a key in the

lock of the street-door, a foot upon the stair, and her husband burst into the room. He looked with surprised inquiring glances from one of us to the other. With a great cry Bertha sprang into his arms, her face upon his shoulder.

"So you have forgiven me, dear William! you have come back!" she said in broken accents.

"Come back!" he replied; "of course I have. What ever is the matter, my love?—you got my message, didn't you?—and the turkey's in the passage, I see. You've paid for it, haven't you?"

"Paid for it!—O, William! Yes! no—what do you mean?"

"Please, ma'am," said the servant-girl, who came in at that moment, "I wished to tell you as the man that have brought the turkey he's my fust-cousin, and I asked him to step into the kitchen, ma'am, till sech times as you was recovered sufficient for to pay for it."

"I'll go and see to it," said I, and went out of the room, leaving the young couple together.

MRS. RALPH GREENING'S FIRST LODGER.

By Arthur Locker.

—o—

ISS VIRGINIA GREENING presents her compliments to the Editor of the *Savage-Club Papers,* and will he kindly permit the accompanying narrative to appear in his widely-circulated pages? Although not herself a member of that renowned coterie, she distinctly recollects a great-uncle, Benjamin Greening, Physician-Extraordinary to his late Majesty King George the Third, who in his youth accompanied Dr. Johnson and Mr. Savage to the Club, and passed a most delightful evening there. She remembers having heard that on this occasion the Doctor sang his famous song 'And so says Mrs. Johnson,' which excited peals of merriment. Miss Greening will feel highly obliged by the Editor's consent, as there are ramifications of her family scattered all over the world, and she wishes them to read the genuine account of an unfortunate occurrence which has been shamefully misrepresented.

Miss Greening is at home every afternoon at five o'clock, and will be most happy to see the Editor, or any of his *collaborateurs*. Tea and coffee are always provided.

Bruton-street, Mayfair, October 18—.

The Greenings are an ancient and honourable family. Our name is unmistakably Saxon; we did not come over with the Conqueror—we were here before him. We remained rather sulky for a couple of hundred years after the Battle of Hastings, as befitted sturdy Englishmen; but at length loyally attached ourselves to the service of the Plantagenet kings. My ancestor Ralph Grenynge was the archer who carried the famous message from Edward the Third to the Black Prince at the Battle of Cressy: "Let the child win his spurs, and let the day be his!" My ancestor Lionel Grenynge was in Henry the Seventh's Exchequer, and many a time has assisted that avaricious monarch to count his money. Another Ralph Greeninge—observe the gradual change of spelling—was Deputy Almoner of the Stone Scullery under the Virgin Queen, and in that capacity rode between Drake and Frobisher to Tilbury Fort (the Southend Railway was not then open) in the eventful year 1588.

But the time would fail me to tell of all the official services performed by the Greening family. One was Governor of Lundy Island; another (of Republican tendencies) carried General Cromwell's spyglass at the Battle of Dunbar; another mended the pen with which the Peace of Ryswick was signed; another, when grouse-shooting in the neighbourhood, was eye-witness to the Chevalier's landing at Moidart; another stood by Captain Cook's side on the fatal shore of Owhyhee. What more need I say? The present generation of Greenings are equally distinguished. Three of them are in the Army, seven in the Church, and fifteen of them in various branches of the Civil Service. Have I not, then, a right, as aunt to the late Ralph Podmore Greening, to take up my pen for the purpose of denying the following atrocious scandal, which please, Mr. Editor, to print in italics: *A member of the Greening family is gaining her livelihood by letting furnished lodgings to criminals!* This intelligence has already penetrated to the East Indies. My cousin, Bob Greening, Cantonment Magistrate at Kumaon, has written two full sheets about it, *viâ* Marseilles. "What is the real truth about this discreditable affair?" he asks indignantly.

For the benefit, therefore, of the various branches

of the Greening family, and of the public at large, I purpose telling all I know of the matter; and, the better to accomplish my object, will begin at the beginning.

People say that I am proud, and have an absurd veneration for purity of blood. I plead guilty to the charge, and have never ceased to regret my brother William's marriage. You may remember, my dear relatives (I am addressing the Greening brotherhood), that he married Sophia Podmore, only daughter of Podmore and Pundle, the great soap-boilers at Rotherhithe. I never thought the Podmore blood would do us any good. My brother William died, leaving five children. I need say nothing of the others. I shall simply follow the fortunes of my favourite nephew — Ralph. He was a well-disposed gentlemanlike boy, in spite of the Podmore blood, and might have done well, had not that silly old Lady Podmore — Sir Samuel was knighted, you may recollect, for presenting his late Majesty with the freedom of the City in a soap-dish — had not that silly old Lady Podmore died, and left Ralph nine thousand pounds. I certainly liked Lady P. She was very good-natured, but she was vulgar and silly, and effected my nephew's ruin by means of that fatal bequest. He quitted the University of Cambridge without taking his degree, which was the more provoking, because his tutor, the Reverend Isaac Tofts, assured me that he never knew a young man with such a head for pure mathematics: it was to an ancestor of mine—George Greening, Fellow of Caius College, and not to that palavering Frenchman Pascal—Rascal, I think it should be—that Sir Isaac Newton was indebted for his theory of gravitation. To return to Ralph. He made no attempt to follow any profession, but wandered in an objectless manner up and down the continent of Europe; while at the premature age of twenty-two he married the eldest daughter of a small and struggling draper, with nine in family, at Beccles in Norfolk.

The news came upon our quiet *ménage* in Bruton-street like a thunderbolt: *Mr. Ralph Podmore Greening, Mrs. Ralph Podmore Greening*, and on the envelope, *Sarah Sabrina Welsh*.

"Let us thank Providence," I said at length, addressing my poor sister Carry, who sat the picture of grief, with her teacup trembling in her hand, " that Ralph has done no worse. He might have married a foreigner; she is at any rate an Englishwoman, and, I trust, a member of the Anglican Church."

"Sadly vulgar, I fear," murmured Carry, with her salts to her darling nose.

"Let us suspend our judgment, dear, till we see her," I replied.

With all his weaknesses, and in spite of the

Podmore blood, Ralph was a Greening, and a gentleman. After the honeymoon he wrote us a very nice note, asking permission to bring his wife to call upon us. We assented, but our misgivings were terrible. I fully expected to encounter a young person whose charms would be most fitly described by the vulgar adjective "blowsy." I was agreeably disappointed—is that correct English, Mr. Editor? Mrs. Ralph proved to be a timid little blushing creature, with a soft gentle voice. I actually might have mistaken her for a lady, had I not been aware of her parentage. Of course she was pretty—boys of two-and-twenty must have good looks—but I had expected a different sort of beauty. She had soft dark eyes and brown hair, a very fair complexion, and a trim little figure. I am ashamed to confess—and Carry and I nearly quarrelled over it—that I fell in love with Mrs. Ralph before she had been half an hour in my company.

Perhaps, however, it was as well that I did so, for a pair of more helpless babies never plighted troth to each other. Ralph answered an advertisement inviting him to speculate in Australian copper mines. He accepted the offer, and in three years had lost every farthing of Lady Podmore's bequest. He was too shamefaced to apply to his friends for assistance, or I have no doubt Sir Lewis Greening, who is hand and glove with the

C—l S—t—y, would have got him some snug governorship in the West Indies, instead of which the foolish creature buried himself in a barbarian quarter of London, called the New North-road, where I discovered him, with an immense vulgar brass plate on his door, selling wine and coals on commission! I persuaded Sir Lewis to buy some of his coals, but they turned out very slaty; while as for his wine, Colonel Greening of the —th, who ordered a few dozen for the mess, says that they were obliged to make a present of it to the non-commissioned officers on St. Patrick's day, and that an Irish sergeant said it went down fairly enough when its flavour was disguised with plenty of whisky.

Poor Ralph was getting into a bad way, and Carry and I, though our means are but small, were privately allowing his wife ten shillings a week, when he caught a severe cold, from standing all day in the rain among the coal-trucks at King's-cross—poor dear creature!—and died.

As soon as the first burst of grief was over, the poor little widow had to think about gaining a livelihood for herself and her two babies. She could not return to her parents, for her father had failed in business, and was living on the charity of his friends. I afterwards learnt that though a draper by trade, his mind was absorbed in geological pursuits, and that he was always willing to desert Horrocks's longcloths for the chance of securing an ammonite or a trilobite.

Mrs. Ralph revolved various schemes in her pretty little helpless head. She would do mantle-making and shoe-binding for the shops, she would advertise for musical pupils, she would get a sewing machine. At length somebody whispered in her ear, " Why not let lodgings? a mint of money may be made by letting lodgings!"

My family pride was sorely wounded when I reflected that a person who bore our honoured name, and in whose children's veins the Greening blood (though diluted with the inferior fluids of Podmore and Welsh) was actually flowing, should be about to engage in this humiliating avocation; but Necessity has no Laws, as Sir Lewis observed in Latin when he kindly gave me a cheque for twenty-five guineas,— for I went begging all round the family, and raised a very pretty little sum.

I persuaded Mrs. Ralph to settle in a somewhat more accessible part of London than the New North-road, and she ultimately took a small house in Duberly-square, in the N.-W. district, *a highly respectable*, but *thoroughly middle-class* locality.

And now, after this prolonged but absolutely necessary exordium, it becomes my duty to narrate the real occurrences which led to the circulation of those shameful rumours—rumours which have even penetrated so far as to poison the peace of families resident under the shadow of the Himalayas—I allude to the Cantonment Magistrate at Kumaon.

Sabrina—for I am so fond of Mrs. Ralph that, though the daughter of a mere retail tradesman, whose family annals fade into ignominious obscurity as soon as you reach the grandfather, I frequently address her by her Christian name—Sabrina kept but one maid. I perceive that this is an inelegant sentence, the parenthesis is longer than the what's-his-name, but I cannot pause over errors of grammar. My feelings are too deeply stirred—the honour of the Greening family is at stake. Sabrina kept but one maid. Her name was Fox, Matilda Fox, an honest, hardworking, faithful, but somewhat eccentric young person. Her manner was far more familiar than we should have tolerated in Bruton-street, and her accent was exceedingly vulgar. With my own ears I heard her *shout* the following information from the area for her young mistress's benefit: "*Hi'm a going hout, and we don't want nothin' from nobody.*" But I can excuse this rude familiarity, and also pardon the discordant hues visible in her bonnet, when I reflect that she was born and bred in Mile End, and until the age of fifteen had never been farther west than Aldgate pump! What a benighted existence! She was large in person, strong-armed, pleasant-looking, but not at all beautiful.

The children adored her; little Mrs. Ralph was rather afraid of her.

Enough of Matilda Fox's characteristics. Let me go on to say that the house was nicely furnished, and a bill announcing that apartments were to be let was exhibited in the window. It was the month of October, and the usual October phenomena were visible. The days were drawing in, Berkeley-square was strewed with dead leaves, our drawing-room fire was lighted, and Sir Lewis had returned from Scotland to Old Palace-yard. But I am straying from the N.-W. district. Several persons had called during the day at Sabrina's house, but as none of them had engaged her lodgings, the foolish creature became quite desponding, although she had only embarked in the business about eight hours before. At length, just at dusk, "between the lights," as my housemaid expresses it, a loud and sonorous rat-tat-tat-tat sounded at the door. Matilda flew upstairs from the kitchen, while Mrs. Ralph hid herself in the parlour. On the steps stood a tall stout man, with a good deal of hair upon his features. "Quite the gentleman"—Matilda presently informed her mistress, but she afterwards acknowledged that she would have liked his looks better if he had not been so closely buttoned up—she would have preferred a more liberal exhibition of linen. He carried nothing in his hand but a small brown-paper parcel, and spoke in a loud authoritative voice, like a "hofficer."

"Haw!" he began, as he pulled his moustache. "Are you the mistress or the servant?"

"The servant, sir," answered Matilda.

"Haw! I never like dealing with servants. Call your mistress."

So Mrs. Ralph appeared from behind the parlour door, blushing with excitement. The stranger pulled off his hat, and made her an exaggerated bow.

"Madam," he said, abandoning the haughty tone with which he had crushed Matilda, and speaking with an air of easy condescension—"Madam, I'm an officer of Engineers, and I want a sitting-room and bedroom. If I like your apartments, I shall stop six months. In a day or two you'll see a 'crow's nest' on that church yonder. We're going to make a military survey of Camden Town."

The lodgings were then examined, and appeared exactly suited to the officer's requirements.

"Have my instruments come?" he suddenly said to Matilda.

"No, sir, nothing's come as I know of."

"Confound those optical scoundrels, they're always behind time! An Engineer officer's nowhere without his theodolite. Lucky I left my luggage at the Langham. I fear I can't take your lodgings, madam," he said to Sabrina.

"O, sir," sighed Mrs. Ralph in a tone of disappointment.

"Well," he remarked relentingly, "perhaps I'd better stop now I'm here. But you must make me very comfortable, madam."

"That I'm sure we'll do," said Sabrina.

"You mustn't let the children annoy me. I've been very nervous ever since I went through the Indian Mutiny."

"They shall be always kept downstairs, sir."

"Very well, I agree to stop a week on trial."

Sabrina looked joyous. Matilda nudged her mistress and whispered:

"You ain't asked him for his reverences."

"O, it's the custom, I believe, sir," began the little woman, hesitating and blushing, "to give some—some reference."

"Reference! Ha! ha!" burst out the stranger jovially, "I can give you a dozen. I hardly know where to begin. My own name, Captain Greville of the Engineers, is a pretty good reference; but perhaps you'd better send round to my friend Lord John Haycock, of the Albany, Piccadilly; or Sir Paul Packingham, at the Grosvenor; or—"

He poured forth such a list of fine names that Mrs. Ralph was quite overcome, and expressed herself perfectly satisfied. Matilda was less credulous, and was about to state her suspicions, when Captain Greville said:

"Now, we Engineers are very particular about our eating and drinking. Everything must be of the very best. Let me have a good dinner in two hours, and bring me up at once a bottle of sherry and soda-water. D'ye hear, girl?"

These last words were addressed to Matilda, in whose eye there lurked a rebellious expression.

"Go at once, Matilda," said Mrs. Ralph, "and fetch everything that the gentleman requires."

Captain Greville was so much pleased with his dinner that he sent for Mrs. Ralph, and gravely complimented her on her excellent housekeeping. "But," said he, somewhat severely, as he held up a table-fork, "we Engineers are accustomed to eat off silver. I wonder that a lady of your position uses electro-plate—it's very vulgar. I hate shams. Have you no silver?"

"I have half-a-dozen tea-spoons," replied Mrs. Ralph meekly.

"Let me have silver at my breakfast," says the Captain.

"Indeed, he sha'n't have nothing of the kind," cried Matilda stoutly, when she and her mistress were in the kitchen together. "I don't believe in that captain, with all his Lord Toms and Sir Harrys. Do you know what he had in that parcel? Nothing but a dirty brush and comb; and I never see nobody that deserved to be called a gentleman so buttoned-up indoors. I don't believe he's got a—"

Next morning the captain asked for the silver spoons.

"They ain't cleaned yet, sir; and I ain't got no whitening," answered Matilda curtly.

Captain Greville made a gesture of annoyance, but remained silent. Immediately after breakfast he said:

"Bring me a flat-iron."

"A flat-iron!" asked Matilda, with a stare.

"Yes," replied the captain with dignity, "a flat-iron. I want it to put on the corner of my trigonometrical plans while I'm drawing."

"Wouldn't a weight be more handy, sir? We've a two-pound weight in the pantry."

"I told you to bring a flat-iron;—bring it."

"Triggery medical plans indeed!" observed Matilda to her mistress. "I don't believe he's got anything of the sort. Why does he want the flat-iron hot? I popped in five minutes afterwards, and there it was between the bars."

There was certainly a good deal of singularity in Captain Greville's behaviour. He talked largely of the extent of his baggage—two cab-loads' he affirmed—but he never sent for it; he stayed indoors all day, and only went out in the evening;

no visitors called upon him; if on the stairs when any of the sterner sex chanced to be coming up—the glazier, for instance, or the upholsterer with the curtain-pole—he retired swiftly to his own chamber; he kept his bedroom-door locked the whole forenoon, and when Matilda was allowed to enter it, the atmosphere smelt strongly of soap-suds and dirty linen; he kept all the drawers locked, although the only outward and visible signs of luggage which he possessed were his hair-brush and comb.

Day after day passed away. The captain lived like a fighting-cock, as Matilda expressed it, on Mrs. Ralph's cookery, and spent the remainder of his indoor life, when not asleep, in smoking cigars and drinking sherry. Day after day Matilda remonstrated with her mistress, saying:

"I'm sure he's no good; he's got no luggage; and you've never seen the colour of his money."

At length, at the end of the week, the captain rang his bell sharply.

"My bill!"

Mrs. Ralph's foolish little heart fluttered with delight.

"I knew he was a gentleman," she said.

Matilda only tossed her head in reply.

The bill was made out, and taken upstairs by the landlady herself. The captain carefully scrutinised the several items.

"Very well, Mrs. Greening," he said at length. "I always like to settle these things at once. Will you have a cheque, or—"

Mrs. Ralph was about to say that she would willingly take a cheque, when the captain continued:

"No, I think I'll pay you in cash; so I'll just step across the street, and change a twenty-pound note."

One, two, three hours elapsed, and the captain did not return. Matilda went upstairs and examined his apartment. His hair-brush and comb had disappeared, which she thought a bad sign, as, besides the clothes on his back, they were the only visible property of which he appeared to be possessed.

The same evening there sounded a peremptory knock at the door. Two keen-eyed gentlemen, dressed like farmers, stood there.

"Got a tall stout gentleman lodging here?" they asked Matilda.

"He's gone hout, and I don't believe he's hever coming in again."

"What makes you think that?"

"Because he's a regular 'umbug. My missis has fed him and lodged him for a week, and never had a halfpenny of money from him."

"It's our man, sure enough," said one of the visitors.

"What d'ye mean by 'our man,' sir?" asked Matilda.

"I mean a man as we want very perticklerly, for half a dozen reasons—for a plate-robbery at Pimlico; for a watch-robbery at Shoreditch Station; for a portmanteau-robbery at the Langham Hotel."

"O, gentlemen," cried Matilda, "ketch me, I'm agoing to faint!" And as she spoke she sank into the detectives' arms. "To think that we've been a 'arbouring such a villain. But what beats me most is that, after all his rogueries, he should be so short of shirts!"

I have given this conversation verbatim, Mr. Editor, as Matilda repeated it to me; and you, I am sure, sir, will excuse the vulgar idiom of this untutored native of the Mile End-road. I have simply desired to state the truth, and to show how it was that a person bearing the honoured name of Greening was reduced to the ignominious necessity of letting lodgings; and how, through her infantine simplicity of character, she extended her first hospitalities to a notorious criminal. Poor thing! Carry and I felt very sorry for her, and made up the loss between us. Silly and helpless as she is, I cannot avoid loving her; indeed, I sometimes regard her as a daughter.

* * * * *

I have just heard the most terrible news. I entirely retract the observation I made about a daughter. For the future, Sarah Sabrina Greening must be a stranger and an alien to us. She is once more engaged to be married!—and to whom? Gracious powers! why, to a middle-aged widower named Biggs, with six children, carrying on an extensive business as a pork-butcher in the Hampstead-road! If the marriage appears in the *Times*, and she advertises herself as widow of the late Ralph Podmore Greening, Carry and I will never forgive her. What a gradual deterioration! Podmores were bad, Welshes worse, Biggses are insufferable. What is to become of those two innocent babes, in whose veins the Greening blood is coursing? Are they to mingle with the offspring of the pork-butcher? I emphatically say, "No!" and darling Carry echoes the observation. We will adopt them.

With the deepest sense of obligation for your exceeding courtesy,

I remain, dear Mr. Editor,
Your obliged and obedient servant,
VIRGINIA GREENING.

The Vision in the Wood.

I.

Escaped the noise and whirl of town,
    The feverish toil, the narrow aim
Of those who struggle for the crown
    Of Fortune or of fleeting Fame,
A wearied mind, a heart bereft
    Of trust and love I with me bore,
Nor sigh'd to quit the land I left,
    Nor smiled to reach the further shore.

II.

And yet that new-found coast was fair—
    A bay where arching aisles of rock
On each hand lift their spires in air,
    And foremost meet the billows' shock.
Behind them winding cliffs expand,
    Bright to the brink with waving grain:
And all the riches of the land
    Salute the splendour of the main.

III.

From thence I gazed on folded hills,
    On wooded vales or orchards meek;
Beside their bounds the tinkling rills
    Reflect the apple's crimson cheek.
Ah me, how once, in scenes like these,
    My heart to Nature's voice had thrill'd,
While by her beauty and her peace
    Each meaner thought was hush'd and still'd!

IV.

'Twas something to lament the past,
    To feel a yearning faint and low
For the sweet glamour fancy cast
    Upon the days of long ago,
As—scanning life's horizon line—
    One mourns a love too early set,
And knows his sorrow more divine
    Than any joy that lingers yet.

V.

Then, 'neath regret for what had flown,
    There stirr'd a tremulous desire
Like the first gleam of embers blown
    Into a fitful transient fire—
A faltering hope that from its death,
    Or seeming death, my soul might rise
Quick with the life of love and faith—
    The life of human sympathies.

VI.

One eve within a tangled wood
    I roam'd ere sunset; pine and oak
And young acacia stemm'd the flood
    Of tidal gold that else had broke
In dazzling glory o'er my course;
    Now, glancing through the leafy shade,
It struck the boughs with soften'd force,
    Or, wavering round the stems, it play'd.

VII.

The woodbine quiver'd in its glow;
    The wild bee, with transfigured wing,
Shone as it rose; the runnel's flow,
    When welling from its darksome spring,
Surprised, grew bright; my spirit, too,
    Issuing from depths of sombre thought,
Met the mild splendour as it flew,
    And sudden gleams of youth recaught.

VIII.

And saw I, by that magic beam,
    The thicket's vista widening yield
And frame a picture like a dream,
    A moving scene—an English field,
An elm-fringed lane, a gabled roof,
    A watching face the casement nigh,
Whose smiles were wrought into the woof
    And warp of all my destiny.

THE VISION IN THE WOOD.

IX.

Through my tranced brain a voice long hush'd
    In subtle music gently wound,
Within my breast old feelings gush'd,
    Responsive to th' invoking sound;
And as a sand-lock'd bark once more
    Rocks 'neath the tide's advancing leap,
My stranded hopes and aims of yore
    Rose buoyant on love's surging deep.

X.

The twilight fell, an amber rain
    Of moonlight steep'd the holy spot—
Did sense deceive? did fancy feign?—
    Methought a Presence unforgot
Sail'd from the shadow. Never, sooth,
    Did lovelier mien the sight engage—
Fair as a poet's dream in youth,
    Sweet as its memory in his age.

XI.

If audible utterance then was mine
    I know not; but my spirit cried
To her who from the far confine
    Of bliss had wander'd to my side,
"O, earliest, latest, only love,
    Forgive the heart where thou wast throned
Its lapses from the life above,
    Thy better influence disown'd!

XII.

Forgive me for the scoffer's taunt,
    The worldling's greed of wealth and power,
Or mean supremacies that vaunt
    Their pageant state, their transient hour;
Forgive the doubt of human worth,—
    How could he doubt, who knew thine own?—
Forgive the will that found in earth
    The immortal spirit's goal and zone.

XIII.

Lo, here at thy dear feet I fling
    This sordid self—again aspire,
Again count love a holy thing,
    And duty dearer than desire,
And doing good in humble ways
    A joy beyond the reach of fame,
And right more blest with God to praise
    Than wrong with all the world's acclaim!"

XIV.

The vision waned; I gain'd the steep;
    The moonlit hamlet smiled below;
A path of splendour cross'd the deep—
    From far I caught its musing flow.
With chasten'd heart, and self-accused,
    I bless'd Him, who in forms of sense,
Or grand or lovely, has infused
    For man redeeming influence.

The Vision in the Wood.

XV.

For still, as taught bard's earliest lays,
    A spirit-life in Nature dwells,
And mystic power the soul doth raise
    When sunset fades on ocean swells;
And tender tones from stream and grove
    With life's pathetic memories blend,
And lift the heart through human love
    To Him who is love's source and end.

ARTEMUS WARD AMONG THE SHOSHONES.

BY EDWARD P. HINGSTON.*

"ARRIOR, what do you say? Shall we go to Big Creek?" said Artemus.

"Why not? It must be a queer place to see, and to lecture there will be something droll to do. We will announce *The Pioneer Lecture in the Shoshone Nation*," was my reply.

"We'll do it, Warrior. Only take care to have at the bottom of the bill 'Admission, one scalp; front seats, two scalps.' Noble Warrior, it's agreed to. Let's take a drink."

It was a playful idea of poor Artemus to call me "Warrior." Before leaving Sacramento for

---

* Mr. Hingston was poor Ward's travelling companion during his expedition to the Mormon Territory—his trusted friend till death. I am glad to have, from his pen, this account of an incident of their travel to which Artemus often alluded.—ED.

Salt Lake City, both he and I had rendered ourselves fully acquainted with the questionable character of the Indian tribes through whose territories we had to pass. Friends who had recently made the journey advised us to provide ourselves with good pistols, and to be always ready in case of a fray. We both bought revolvers. Artemus, with characteristic eccentricity, persisted in carrying his unloaded in his portmanteau—the ammunition in one corner, the pistol in another; whilst I, with a due regard for the exigencies which might arise, displayed the latest edition of Colt conspicuously in my belt, just as other travellers were accustomed to do. Hence the pleasant banter of my being addressed as "Warrior."

Our journey was made in the winter of 1863-4. The conversation above recorded took place at Austin, Reese River, Nevada Territory, nearly two hundred miles from any town we had left behind us, and four hundred from the next to which we were advancing. We were in the heart of the Shoshone land. Behind and before us were Indian tribes of the very worst classes of Indians; beings rightly representing the savage in all the lawlessness, cruelty, dirt, and degradation belonging to the aborigine of the western wilderness. Neither Artemus Ward nor myself were saplings enough to imagine that we were about to meet the noble heroes of Fenimore Cooper. Uncas is

about as mythical as Actæon, and Chingachkook as
legendary as Ulysses. Mr. Hepworth Dixon, in
his recent journey to Utah, fell in with representatives of many of the Indian nations ; but he did
not travel south enough to see the most objectionable, nor west enough to meet the most degraded.
We had been amongst the *Digger* tribe of California, than whom lower types of humanity can
hardly be imagined ; the *Cricks* and *Snakes* of
Nevada, than whom none are more wily and
more treacherous ; and we were now among the
Shoshones, who, if not the most to be dreaded,
are certainly the laziest and dirtiest. It has been
asserted of them—how truthfully I know not—that
they have no idea of a Deity, nor any belief in the
existence of a *great Spirit*. Thoroughly nomadic
in their habits, they roam from place to place ; feed
on fruits, roots, and game ; dress themselves in
filthy skins ; cut their hair straight across the forehead, and tie pieces of old iron to it at the sides ;
make their women do all the work ; are polyga-
mous as Mormons in their marital notions ; and
when they die have their wives killed and buried
with them. Amongst these gentle creatures we
found ourselves at Austin.

A strange place was Austin in 1863. To get
to it we had left California, scaled the Sierra Nevada, visited the wondrous silver mines of Virginia
City and Washoe, traversed the sterile desert of

Nevada, crossed the " sink" of the Carson, where a river becomes absorbed and disappears abruptly in an arid waste ; stopped at stations to change mules, where the poor fellows who had charge of the station were expecting hourly an Indian attack ; and we were now some four thousand feet above the level of the sea, five hundred miles from the Pacific coast, high up in the Toiyabe range of mountains, with nothing but wild country, wild beasts, and wild Indians away to the north, and little else but wilder Indians, wilder beasts, and wilder country away to the south ; desert in any quantity to the west, and desert in greater quantity to the east. We had plenty of fresh air.

Arrangements had been made for Artemus Ward to lecture in Austin, the Court-house having been retained for that purpose—a rough wooden building, stuck upon piles, by the side of a hill. The miners had agreed to bring their own chairs and stools with them. But previous to our amusing the Austin folks there was just one evening to spare, and that Artemus desired to devote to Big Creek, a mining village about twelve miles distant, and of only a few months' growth. Why he wished to go to Big Creek was simply because it was the wildest place he could go to for lecturing purposes. Big Creek was on the very edge of the wilderness ; Big Creek had never had an entertainment of any kind ; and Big

Creek owned a mingled population of three parts miners and one part Shoshone Indians. No one else would have thought of lecturing there; and that was the very reason why Artemus Ward wished to go.

We "liquored up" at the International Hotel, an establishment constructed partly of wood and partly of canvas. We had also taken apartments there for sleeping. They consisted of two shelves, one above the other, in a room where there were eight or ten other shelves separated by linen partitions. The floor was of hard mud, the roof of boards, through the holes in which the wind whistled and the rain fell.

"This is pretty rough," observed Artemus; "surely they cannot have anything rougher in Big Creek!"

"Well, I guess they have," remarked Mr. William Albaugh, a stout miner, who stood at the bar beside us. "They're mighty rough over thar. If you are going over thar to lecture, you'll have to do it in the 'Young America Saloon,' and thar you'll see something; and you'll have to get thar over some very queer country, and thar you'll see something; and you'll find no beds thar, and have to ride back at night, when maybe you may see something too."

"Any noble savages about?" inquired Artemus.

"Shoshones? Yes, plenty; and not an honest Injun among them."

"Not much worse, I suppose, than that majestic child of freedom chopping wood in the road?" suggested Artemus, pointing to an Indian who, clad in a filthy fur, was cutting up firewood in front of the hotel for the use of the inmates.

"Worse than he?—worse than Buffalo Bill? ay, a thousand times. And he'd as soon tomahawk you as cleave that wood, if he dared. Mr. Ward, can you fight? are you armed?" asked Mr. William Albaugh very seriously.

Artemus replied that he was; and as for fighting, he presumed that he could do his share. But the impressiveness of Mr. William Albaugh made the Indian question serious. Our conversation had attracted the attention of some half-dozen loiterers in the bar, including a miner by the name of Marshall, and a stout, merry, red-faced man, who held the position of Wells and Fargo's Express agent.

"If you make up your mind to go to Big Creek, Mr. Ward," said the agent, "I would advise you to hire a black horse they have in the stables behind, put him in a strong buggy, and drive across. If any rascally Indians come in your way, drive all the harder."

Artemus Ward meditated for a few minutes;

then, taking me aside, he pointed to Buffalo Bill, who was still chopping the wood. "Hingston," said he, "there's not much to fear from such fellows as that. Besides, if we jib on going a journey of twelve miles because of Indians, what's the use of our attempting to travel a thousand miles to the Rocky Mountains? Have your revolver ready, old Warrior, and we'll do Big Creek, if only for the fun of it. 'The Pioneer Lecture in the Shoshone Nation, by the Wild Humorist of the Plains;' that's the title. Never mind the Indians. Come along."

Every mining town of two hundred inhabitants "out west" has a newspaper-office. The *Reese-River Reveille* was the name of the one in Austin. There we succeeded in getting a dozen small posters printed; and having sent them on ahead, we started for Big Creek. Our start was an event of sufficient importance to draw together a large assemblage, composed of miners, Indians, coach-drivers, and "loafers." Buffalo Bill, the wood-chopper, his axe on his shoulder, stood the centre of a group of the wildest-looking Shoshones, all of them intently regarding our preparations for departure. When we had taken our seats in the buggy and gathered our furs around us, Mr. William Albaugh handed up a bottle of Bourbon whisky and a glass.

"Take a good hoist," said he. "Keep to the

track through the sage-brush. Have your pistols ready, and look out for Injuns."

"Shoshones are thieving critturs, everyone of them," remarked Marshall the miner.

"Gentlemen, a pleasant drive to you, and take care to bring your scalps back to Austin," was the prudent advice of the Express agent.

Artemus replied to them all by imitating the wild screech of the Indian. Then off we drove through the grand mountain-gorge in which Austin is situated. High up in the sides of the hills were the huts of the silver miners, and away down in the valley were the roughly-constructed mills for crushing the silver ore. There were a thousand people in Austin; six months before there were not ten. Silver had done it all. The rocks on each side of us we knew to be full of silver; the road over which we drove was seamed with silver ore; and as we descended through Marshall's Canon to Clifton, the plains of Silver Land opened out to us, covered with stunted sage-brush, dreary, treeless, and desolate,—the cheerless basin of some ancient sea, the very waters of which would seem to have been liquid silver in the earth's first morn of being.

Our course was to the south, almost parallel with Reese River, having the river to our right and a range of mountains to our left. The plain was partially covered with snow. No Indians nor anything living was to be seen, nor any vegetation except tufts of the scraggy, gray-coloured sage-brush, the most forlorn and unpicturesque of vegetable formations. Here and there deep gulches crossed our track; but otherwise the road was pretty good, and not difficult to be traced through the thin coating of snow.

Big Creek was arrived at in due time, and the lecture delivered that evening. Our lecture-hall was a large bar-room, the roof of which was formed of pine-branches, supported by pillars of roughly hewn pine-logs. The seats were formed of planks resting on old barrels and wheelbarrows. Every miner had heard of Artemus Ward. Big Creek turned out enthusiastically to listen to the story of the *Babes in the Wood*. The price of admission was three dollars each (twelve shillings). We had an audience of nearly a hundred-and-fifty miners, wearing gray shirts and large slouch hats. Artemus stood up on one end of the bar to talk, while the process of liquor-serving went on industriously at the other end.

The lecture was over before nine o'clock, and, after partaking of a hasty supper and some whisky, we prepared to leave. Our hospitable friends supplied us liberally with cigars, and insisted on our taking a demijohn of whisky with us in the buggy. They also furnished us with a lamp and a box of matches; for though the night was fine at present, there were signs of a storm coming on.

"Did you see William Albaugh in Austin?" asked the landlord of the Young America Saloon, "and did he give you any caution about the Indians?"

"He did," replied Artemus; "but there was not a sign of an Indian all along the road."

"You might meet with them to-night, though. Don't go unless you've made up your minds to. We can find you a bed. If you do meet with Indians, keep a stiff upper-lip, and your hand on your pistol. The Shoshones are an awful lot."

Artemus had no fear. Poor fellow, he never had. He was determined to go back to Austin that night; and though I timidly suggested it would be wiser to stop where we were, he was resolute on going.

There was sufficient moonlight at the starting to enable us to see our way nicely through the creek, and we were soon out upon the open plain. For the first three or four miles we bowled along rapidly over the crisp snow, amongst the crackling sage-brush. Then the moon became hidden by clouds; there was no light. We had to trust to the horse.

"Where the plague have we got to?" suddenly cried out Artemus, who was driving. "Get out, Hingston, and see. Light the lantern."

I did so, and it was well that I did. We were almost at the edge of a perpendicular bank, full twelve feet high, at the bottom of which was an inlet of Reese River. A few yards more, and we should have toppled over headlong. The precipitous character of the gulch showed that we had driven too far to the left, and ought to have crossed the small stream higher up.

Lantern in hand, I led the way over the snow to where we could find a fit place for crossing. It was too dark to drive fast; so I picked out the road with the lantern, and Artemus walked the horse after me, until, arriving at a fordable place, we passed over the stream, found ourselves once more on the snow-covered plain, and I resumed my place in the buggy.

"Hide that confounded lamp between your knees, and let me make out, if I can, where we are driving," said Artemus suddenly. "It seems to me that there is a light ahead. What is it, my Warrior?"

I looked, and sure enough in the distance there was the gleam of what appeared to be a fire. How a fire should happen to be there, unless some one was encamped for the night, was more than we could guess. We commenced discussing the question whether it was likely to be a party of miners or a party of Indians, when the horse stumbled, the buggy capsized, and we found ourselves in a ditch, one of our shafts broken, and the lantern lost.

"Confound the road!" was my friend's exclamation, at the same time laughing heartily at our disaster. "Let us make for that light in the distance, whatever it is. You lead the horse, and I'll feel the way. The light must be from a fire. We shall get a warming, if we get nothing else."

Artemus affected to be careless of results; but the silence he kept, as he paced on in advance, was evidence of his anxiety. We were approaching the light, which manifestly proceeded from a fire behind a piece of rising ground not far in front of us. As we neared it, we heard a slight rustle in the sage-brush beside us, and in a moment two dusky figures rose out of the darkness and stood before us on our path.

There was no mistaking them. Dark as the night was, their outlines were clearly discernible. They were Indians!

Before I could draw my pistol, my arm was pinioned in a tight grip. Artemus was seized upon in a similar manner. Our captors at once gave a loud yell, which was answered by another of a similar kind from more Indians on the other side of the rising ground.

Neither Artemus nor I attempted to resist. The suddenness of the seizure had paralysed us both. Trembling and shivering, we allowed the Indians to lead us to the fire, grouped around which were five other Indians, dimly distinguishable in the dusky light, but each with his face painted, his long black hair straggling over it, and each armed with a rifle, the muzzle of which was instantly turned upon us. In front of the fire were two large scalping-knives, placed there, as it seemed, to be warmed, their blades reflecting the firelight with a sickening gleam.

Our captors motioned us to kneel down upon the earth, keeping guard over us with their rifles, while their five comrades retreated a little into the shade.

After half an hour or more of silence, during which my blood seemed to trickle coldly through my veins, and we both remained almost motionless, an Indian on the other side of the fire gave a wild whoop, brandished his tomahawk, leapt over the smouldering ashes, and, alighting in front of Artemus, demanded, in scarcely understandable English, his name.

"Artemus Ward," very tremblingly spoken.

"Wh-r-r-r-r-ah-e! Uo, uo, uo.* Americano talkee-man," cried the Indian, running his forefinger round each of our scalps, and imitating the process of scalping.

* "Yes, yes, yes," in the Shoshone language.

"Talkee, talkee!" chimed in the others, as if addressing Artemus.

"What do they want?" asked my friend of me very anxiously.

"They want you to speak to them. Say something, for Heaven's sake!"

"My good Indian friends," commenced Artemus, "I am a peaceful man. I—"

"Wh-r-r-r-r-r-ah-e!" cried another of the Indians, skipping forward with a bottle in his hand, and offering it to Artemus. "Whisky— *devite, devite*. Drinky—lecture—talkee!"

"What do they want me to do?" asked Artemus of me.

"They want you to drink some whisky. *Devite* is Shoshone for 'good.' They must know you, for they require you to get up on that bank and lecture to them. Pray do it; do anything to please them."

We both took a drink from the proffered bottle. It did not escape my notice that, as Artemus put the bottle to his lips, his eyes rested very searchingly upon the stoutest Indian of the party, the one whose face was painted the most, and who had the most genial expression, though the most uncouth attire.

Giving back the bottle, Artemus stepped up on the bank beside the fire, and, in the coolest manner, commenced to talk:

"Noble Shoshones! Brave and heroic warriors of a mighty race! The constitution of the United States was framed by the great and glorious George Washington. He wrote it out at tea-time over a bottle of Bourbon and a hot cornmeal cake. He wrote in that glorious document that the Shoshone nation should ever be respected. He wrote, did that great and good man, that—"

"Bosh!" cried one of the Indians, in very good and very distinct English.

At the same moment a whisky-bottle was thrown at Artemus, breaking into twenty pieces as it fell at his feet.

The lecturer gave one glance at the stout Indian, whom he had noticed so intently a few minutes previously, jumped quickly from the bank, dashed at the savage, seized his long black hair, and tearing it away, revealed, when reft of their disguise, the unmistakable features of Mr. William Albaugh.

Almost at the same moment I recognised in my captor the face of Buffalo Bill.

A loud whoop from Artemus, and a louder burst of laughter from the Indians, was followed by Marshall the miner, and Wells and Fargo's Express agent, also divesting themselves of their Indian head-dress, and shaking us very heartily by the hands.

"Gentlemen, we apologise for the scare we

have given you," said Mr. William Albaugh. "Let it be a lesson to you to be careful how you travel in Indian territory. We have waited for you out on the plain till we have got well chilled. Buffalo Bill, stir up the fire, set some water boiling, and let's all have a whisky-toddy."

We had some, and in an hour afterwards were on our road to Austin.

The Magical Ointment.

By HAIN FRISWELL.

On the shores of the Red Sea, just where they fish for pearls, and sell to the outer barbarians of the West, and the Frankish unbelievers in the glorious Prophet—blessed be his name!—the spoil of a shell-fish, there lived a poor merchant, who, never having had a good chance in his life, was therefore virtuous, though somewhat bitter against those whose chances were better. Do what he could, he never managed to get rich, great, or respected; and he well knew that if he achieved the first, the second or third would be sure to follow.

Our friend Hadji Beidâwi read in the Korân three times a day, and performed his ablutions seven times; but no diver ever brought to him the large pearls, beautiful as the moon and resplendent as the silver stars. Oftentimes, poor man, he would speculate upon the chances, and buy the contents of a boat—in conjunction with other merchants—but the fish withheld their treasures, and were mostly empty, or the pearls were as black as the tongue of a liar, or as the teeth of him who devours the betel-nut. At another time the Hadji Beidáwi would ride forth and meet the *Pillal Karras*, the binder of sharks—a mysterious priest from Malabar—who, knowing that the Hadji was descended from a holy man, who had written a commentary on the one great book, would tell him all his secrets, and whether the *Djinns* would allow the boats to go out. If the *Pillal* shook his head, and intimated that there would be no catch, then the Hadji would hasten back and stake his money against the market; but he always lost. Then he tried a disbelief in the holy man, and placed his money in the reverse way advised, and with precisely the same result to him. Next he bought a slave, a diver, and sent him (for he was known to be lucky, and well reputed for courage and sagacity) all naked to the troubled waters, urging him, no less by blows than by promise of reward, to bring up a pearl of great value. Alas, the diver, after three or four days of fruitless labour, getting tired and exhausted, and yet driven to work in spite of the predictions of the binder of sharks, became sulky, foolish, and timid, and so fell into the way of the first shark which came near him, and was rendered useless for life by having his right arm bitten off.

The Hadji, with a groan of disappointment, had his slave's bleeding stump cauterised with a red-hot iron, and then sent him forth into the desert, giving him his freedom, since he was for ever useless. Then he wrapped up his head in the folds of his green turban, and sat silent and sulky in his tent, for ruin stared him in the face.

His wife Ayesha—for the Hadji Beidâwi was too poor to keep four wives, and therefore piously contented himself with one—came to bring him a bowl of camel's-milk, and to comfort him.

"O, my master," said she, "lift up your head and look out of the tent, for good-luck cometh this way in the shape of the *Pillal Karras*—beautiful are his feet!"

"Accursed be he!" said Beidâwi; "his legs are but stumps, and his feet as big as those of a camel. He a binder of sharks!—why bound he not the mouth of the one which has rendered my diver useless for ever?"

"Beidâwi, Beidâwi!" said the Pillal, who stood within the tent and heard all; "thrice, in the name of the Prophet, have I saluted thee; and lo, a cloud is on thy face, and thine anger is kindled at thy friend, although I told thee that the sharks were out, and no magic would bind them."

This indeed was true, as the Hadji well knew; but he had lost all faith in the shark-binder, and hated him all the more because he was right. Then the Pillal sat down, and Ayesha gave him to eat of rice that was as snowy as the flower of the myrtle, and of honey yellow as gold; and the heart of the old priest warmed within him.

"Where is thy son Omar?" he asked of Ayesha. "Is he not the prop of the house and the promise of the future, as Isaac was to Abraham?"

The Pillal was a learned man and a traveller. He was also a priest, although employed in this roving commission of binding the sharks and bottling-up the winds; so Ayesha hastened behind the curtain of camel's-skin to bring forward Omar.

"Come here, my son; here is a learned Dervish, who can read and explain the Korân, and copy the ninety-nine names of God; and who says the Fâ-thàt.* He is a servant of the Rabbi 'lâlamîna (the Lord of all creatures), and peradventure will bless thee; therefore come hither."

Omar did as he was told. He was a most modest, innocent, good boy, almost ready to go forth into the world, and was well-grown and of good favour. He came, looking with astonish-

* This forms the first chapter of the Korân, and is the daily prayer of pious Mussulmen. The whole chapter is not so long as our Lord's Prayer, and does not extend to more than five lines of the type of the page before the reader.

ment at his father, who still kept his head covered, and saluted the priest.

"God is knowing and wise," said the Pillal, quoting the Korân; "God desireth to be gracious unto you; turn not away from the truth with a great deviation."

Beidâwi groaned in spirit. How often had he said his prayers, and how utterly had they failed to bring him pearls, riches, mules, white asses, and people who should kiss his stirrups to do him honour!

"What is the use of prayer?" said he.

"God hath indeed promised everyone Paradise," said the imperturbable priest; "but few shall arrive there."

Omar knew that he was quoting the holy book, from his measured and somewhat stilted tone, so he bowed his head piously. Beidâwi bit his tongue with rage, and said nothing.

"Seek not for riches, nor for power, young man," said the priest, speaking at the father, but to the son. "Did not Eblis* seek for power, and did he not fall? 'Worship Adam,' said God to the angels, and they worshipped: but Eblis was not one who worshipped, for he said he was more excellent than Adam, since God created him of

---

* Eblis is the Devil, Satan, or Tempter. This story is told in the seventh chapter of the Korân, entitled Al Arâf—the Partition.

fire, but man of black mud. Then the Great One ordered him into hell, saying, 'Get thee hence; thou art proud, but shalt be as one of the contemptible.' Then Satan said, 'Give me respite till the resurrection.' 'Verily,' said God, 'thou art respited till then.' Then, with a malicious grin, Eblis cried, 'Thou hast depraved me, and I will deprave thy creatures; I will lie in wait for man in the strait path, and beguile him.' Then Allah said, 'Get thee hence, despised; *this too is what I have ordained.*' Yea, God is great; his designs are from the beginning of the world!"

Beidâwi himself, although he knew the sacred writings, was plunged in thought by the relation, and uncovered his head.

"Truly," said the Pillal, "thy heart is warm within thee. I grieve at thy poverty, I grieve for thy slave. Here, take this box. Money I have none; but this is more precious than money, or the glittering dust of the rock. It is not for thee; but it will make the fortune of thy son." So saying, he repeated the Fá-thát, and turning round three times, left the tent.

"An old humbug," said Beidâwi; "what is the use of praying if you don't get money by it? Now, he *does* get money by his prayers. Fortune for my son! alas, 'tis little else he'll have."

He looked at the green box; a box of small dimensions indeed, made of ivory. He would have thrown it in the fire, as we Europeans say, but for two considerations. In the first place, there was no fire in his tent; and secondly, he found on the box a band of paper on which was the name of God and his Prophet, which it would have been an awful offence to burn. So putting it under his pillow, he rolled himself up on his carpet and sulked. "Fortune!" said he. "What an old humbug it is! It can only contain a pearl as big as a small orange. Ah, what a fortune that would be; or two or three diamonds as big as date-stones! But no." Here he shook the box, and found that it did not rattle. Then he looked at the paper, and saw that a little grease, urged by the warmth of his pillow, had oozed forth. "What a rogue it is, this Pillal!" said he. "Here, Ayesha, take the box. You believe in the priests; *I* don't."

So far Beidâwi, who must now depart from this story. The Pillal made his fortune by prayers and jugglery, and went back to Malabar. The various merchants made theirs with pearls, of which many were found; and the unfortunate Hadji caught only a fever, which, made greater by disappointment and mental trouble, killed him in two months; and his faithful wife Ayesha, who was worn out with nursing, only survived him five days, giving with her dying hand to Omar, who stood weeping by her side, the magic box of ointment.

The weeping Omar, bidden to look upon the little green box as his whole fortune, was not very well contented; but he loved his mother with an intense affection, and for many days thought rather of her than of his fortune. He buried both his parents, exhausting the whole of his fortune—or of that little remnant of property they had left him—in the pious process; and then joining himself to some luckier merchant as a servant, went forward to Cairo.

Yes; unto the degraded condition of a servant was the descendant of Abu Beidâwi, the great literary man, the interpreter of the Korân, the wise writer of glosses, reduced. Happily, Omar was, as we have said, of the gentlest and noblest disposition, and it hurt him not to serve. He worked merrily, and did well, and lived for some years with the merchant Yusuf, but grew no richer, and was, indeed, a very poor man. This he cared not for, reading the Korân in a far other spirit than that of the Hadji his father.

Well, when Omar arrived at Cairo, to be sure, he found that it was very different to be poor in the city, and poor on the sea-coast or the desert. A thousand temptations beset him. He began to think with, and to think of, his father. When he saw slaves leading women beautiful as houris, no doubt, but enveloped in mantles, and with nothing to be seen but two great lustrous eyes, he felt that it was well to be rich, since the rich alone could marry. When he saw the Arnaut swagger past him armed to the teeth, and with a black wand in his hand strike away the shrinking poor, he saw it was not well to be poor. He saw fine horses, wondrous houses, Damascus blades, splendid mules, stuffs, dyes, purples, gold, silver, all the charms of life,—and the spirit of his father came to him, and he was sad.

Still he was prayerful and modest. When people spoke to him, he told the truth; when they inquired the price of his services, he asked little; he never pushed forward; he was retiring, shrinking, good, and honest, no praiser of himself. At last he fell in love, and with the daughter of Yusuf, whom he saw one day without her face-veil, as beautiful as the moon.

Then it was that Omar felt the curse of poverty, and turned first on this side, then on that, then on another, to grow rich. But the luck of his father followed him; nothing that he could do aided him. Instead of growing richer and richer, he grew poorer and poorer. His master, perceiving his love, turned him from his doors; and although his honesty was known, yet he could not easily find another situation; for this cause, as there was no apparent reason alleged, there were many suspected.

Mourning, therefore, for his separation from the

beautiful Halima, and melancholy with his many
sad reflections, Omar sat in an obscure caravan-
serai with only two pieces of gold in his pocket,
and with two treasures besides — a small steel
mirror which Halima had given him, — there
were specks of rust on it, and it was becoming
useless, — and the green box of ointment. "My
fortune," said he sadly, as he looked at it;
"would it were worth while to give it to the
beautiful Halima!"

Then he began to think what he should do,
and then again a vision of the old shark-binder
and the rough skin tent of the Hadji Beidâwi
floated before him.

There might be, he thought, a diamond con-
cealed in the ointment, for ointment his mother
had told him it was; if it were a pearl, it would
infallibly have been spoilt. There *might* be a
diamond. His mother, who venerated the name
which covered the box, thought that it had been
given only to keep that name as a charm in the
house. But the spirit of Omar's father, not of his
mother, ruled; and in despite of his pious education he tore off the holy name, scattered it amidst
the dust of the yard and the dung of the camels,
and opened the box.

Father and mother were both right: there was
nothing but green ointment.

Omar felt as if he could throw the box under

the feet of the camels; but he said nothing, but sat gazing in stupid wonder.

Suddenly his nose itched. The truth is, that in turning him somewhat too peremptorily out of doors—a poor servant as he was—for daring to look so ardently at his daughter, Yusuf had clenched his fist, and had, as they say in the chronicles of the Frankish fisticuffers, dealt his servant "a facer." Omar's nose was swollen.

"Allah Akbar!" said Omar with a sigh; "the ointment may be precious ointment, although it be not made of diamonds."

So he rubbed it on his nose, and a wondrous effect it had. His visage became hard, bold-looking, and calm. He lost all his modesty and shamefacedness. The swelling had disappeared; and the feeling produced by the salve was so novel that Omar anointed his cheeks, and they became as brass in their boldness; then under his eyes, and they were no longer downcast, but brilliant, impudent, roguish, bright as stars; then he touched his lips, and they curved into a smile, and began to lie in a wonderful way, and to swear by Allah falsely, and to adjure the Prophet without a reason. Next he rubbed it over his forehead, and it became as marble and as bronze combined.

Omar had now exhausted half of the box; the rest he put by for further occasions; and, admiring his brass face in the steel mirror, which he

threw at the head of a slave who came to ask him
for money, he passed out back to his old quarters,
to the house of Yusuf, fastening a handsome sci-
mitar to his side, and taking up the jewelled and
gold-fringed turban of a feeble old Turk, who was
asleep in one of the best and coolest compartments
of the inn, and putting it on his head.

He did this with such an air, that the bystanders thought he was the traveller's son, and
let him pass out; and when he came to the dwelling of Yusuf, the slaves opened the gates to him,
and did not seem even to know the humble Omar
in the bold, turbulent, handsome Arab officer who
stood before them. They ushered him at once
into the chief office of the jewel-merchant.

Yusuf jumped off his seat, and bowed before
him.

"Look up, old man," said Omar.

"My lord will excuse an humble merchant.
What jewels wish you?"

"Your daughter Halima," returned Omar.

The merchant, with a surprised air, straightened
his backbone and looked at him.

"Omar!" he gasped;—"thou villain! I
thought it was the Sultan himself, or at least the
Vizier. My daughter! Thou—thou shalt suffer
the bastinado!"

But as he looked he trembled, so magical was
the bronzed face of Omar.

"Bastinado, old man!" said Omar. "Beware! Who sold a mere doublet to the Vizier as a sapphire of great price? Who put off French paste as diamonds? Who made me—so modest and humble—his confidant? Who cheated the Father of the Faithful himself in the matter of the measure of seed-pearls?"

Yusuf fell on his knees before Omar. He had his master in his power.

Need I say more? The reader can imagine the ensuing effects of the ointment.

In a short time Omar shared the riches of Yusuf; in a short time too he managed to make his master a beggar, and himself the wealthiest merchant in Cairo. Everywhere his bronzed face served him. He never blushed, he felt no emotion, he had no compunction. He grew rich as Crœsus.

You may fancy that of course he married the girl whom he loved. He did no such thing. He wedded four of the richest and ugliest women he could well find, and diverted the fortunes of their fathers, for they were heiresses, into his own treasury. But the daughter of Yusuf adorned his hârem with many other beauties from Circassia and Nubia.

Omar became a magistrate, the most expeditious ever known; for he always found out who could pay the largest bribe, and he, whether plaintiff or defendant, gained the cause. In short, no Moslem was ever known who was richer, more powerful, or more successful than Omar Beidâwi. Slaves knelt to him and grovelled before him; princes held his stirrup and marvelled at the old man, with his bronzed stern face and his white hair.

At length it was his turn to die; for, however successful we are, die we must. He wiped his clammy brow with a napkin fringed with gold, and, while slaves stood round him, and the best physicians tried to soothe his pains, took from his pillow the magic ointment, and would once more have anointed his face.

Suddenly an old man stood by his side and arrested his hand. Omar turned on him his dying eye, and recognised — bent and brown, but not much older in his looks—the binder of sharks.

"Wretch!" he cried, "who gave me misery, not happiness — thou who hast loaded my soul with guilt — why withhold my hand? I need anointing before I dare behold the face of Allah!"

"*The ointment is of no use there*, not if it were as magical as that of Rabbi Ben Hôllowai!" grinned the old man. "The devil can quote Scripture, and turn it to his purpose; and I am no inferior imp of Eblis. You mistrusted in your own heart; you profaned your prayers, your wishes, and the name of Allah; and you too I met in the strait way, and overthrew. Adieu! The box reverts to its owner. You have had your chances on earth, but, my son, you have missed the thin straight line, the spider's web, on which the faithful — bold in their righteousness, their modesty, goodness, and their true hearts—venture to walk to Paradise."

So saying, he clutched the box, and muttered an incantation in the dying man's ear, as Omar gave up the ghost.

It will be some satisfaction to know that Omar's body was splendidly buried; that the expounders of the Korân went through all their rites, being well paid for it out of his estate; and that the rich, especially those who joined his feasts, and who were *not* left out of sundry bequests, mourned for him; but the poor avoided his grave, for under the cypress that waves over it, it is said that a dreadful Djinn sits mocking in the soft Egyptian nights, holding under the starlight a box of ointment.

ST. ANTHONY PREACHING TO THE FISHES.

St. Anthony's Sermon.

A MEDIÆVAL LEGEND.

By Walter Thornbury.

———o———

I.

St. Anthony in his holy zeal
    Came to the river side,
To preach to the little fishes
    On the wickedness of pride.

II.

The kingfisher was diving
    Down from the willow-stump;
The swallows gay were skimming
    Over the osier-clump;

III.

The bulrushes were nodding
    In an assenting way,
The water-flags were wading
    Out from each shallow bay;

IV.

As the Saint in his long brown mantle
    Down through the osiers came,
And called to all the little fish,
    And summoned them by name.

V.

The dace, in clouds of silver,
    Came clustering in fear;
And after them the gudgeons
    Swam jostling to hear.

VI.

The eels sped twisting, twining,
    Next the perch with his orange fin:
The surly pike and the barbel,
    The bleak so gentle and thin.

VII.

The big trout crimson-spotted,
    Flapping his nimble tail;
And the supple, silvery salmon,
    Cased in his pliant mail.

IX.

He touched not at their special sins,
    But preached of avarice,
Of homicide, and theft, and all
    Those forms of wickedness.

X.

At simony and bigamy
　　He launched full many a text,
Until the finny people
　　Wondered what would come next.

XI.

Then the Saint his congregation
　　Dismissed, and homeward went.
Both the holy man and his hearers
　　Each in their way content.

BILGER'S.

BY GEORGE MANVILLE FENN.

———o———

YOU did not know Bilger's? No, I suppose not; for though it was in a good situation for trade, it stood neither in the Strand nor in Holborn, but, as Mrs. Bilger herself used to say, "betwix and between." And you never will know it now, though you may encounter Mrs. Bilger some time in the future, and I hope that such may be your lot. But Bilger's has gone: it is a thing of the past, and was carried away in the form of bricks in contractors' carts; in a gritty painful dust in wayfarers' eyes; in scraps of lath by boys; blown away in rags of wall-paper by the wind; and the last time I was by that way, there was nothing left of Bilger's but the smell. For, along with street, court, lane, alley, hole, and corner, Bilger's was wanted; and required after a new fashion to be "thrown into Chancery," to be swallowed up by the law—that voracious monster of the insatiable maw; and it, meaning Bilger's—and they, meaning the streets, courts, lanes, alleys, holes, and corners, were knocked down by auctioneers, and pulled down by dusty men, who stood in dangerous places with pickaxes, loosening bricks and mortar, which they sent down in dusty avalanches upon travellers' heads, crying out "below!" to the sufferers, who promptly took the hint to get out of the way; but from the avalanche, and not from the shout, for the latter invariably came too late.

Bilger's is not, for it was wanted for the new Law Courts, and Mrs. Bilger had notice to quit; whereupon she told the bearer that an Englishman's house was his castle, and threw the notice at him. But after the man had shaken the dust of Bilger's from his feet and taken his departure, Mrs. Bilger remembered that though she held the lease of the house in Cress-alley for thirty years unexpired, she was not an Englishman; and besides, although she had her lease, from divers signs of the times she had a shrewd suspicion that the old house would soon come down "neck and crop" (her own words again): so, like a wise woman, she went and consulted her solicitor, Mr. Parch, of Bream's-buildings, into whose den she walked awefully, and holding her bulky umbrella in front, as an unprotected female should. For Mr. Parch's was a serious place for a lone female to enter, and Mrs. Bilger quite shuddered as she glanced up at the grimy gas-pipe running above her head, from which depended a wire bill-file, upon which were impaled a score of dusty writs, like so much legal mistletoe.

But Mrs. Bilger had come upon business, and business was transacted : the magic word " compensation" was rolled out of the treasury of Mr. Parch's knowledge ; and with that word Mrs. Bilger and her solicitor played catch-ball for a quarter of an hour, and then departed the dame ; while for result, some time after, the solicitor presented his bill and a heavy cheque to his client. There was a little writing and signing ; a decanter of sherry produced from a dirty tin box bearing the legend " Bulks's affairs"—Bulk, the wine-merchant, you know, of the Strand, who died of *del. trem.*—and then, mutually satisfied, lawyer and client separated, and Mrs. Bilger, having sold out, gave up her keys. That same day, too, there was a small vanload of furniture went from the end of Pickett-place, with a nest in the top formed of a large feather-bed tied up in a patchwork quilt, and in that nest sat Mrs. Bilger and Tot ; while, after mounting thereto by means of a ladder, Mrs. Bilger said, " Goodness gracious only knew how they were to get down again." But James Stogle, carman, vans at eighteenpence per hour, said "all right, marm," when Mrs. Bilger was satisfied, and complacently surveyed the world from the Strand to Hanwell from her elevated position, even condescending just to wet her lips from Mr. Stogle's pewter pot when the thirsty horses were obliged to be stayed so often upon the road.

Mrs. Bilger lives in a cottage at Hanwell, and takes walks with Tot; but we have more to do with Bilger's of Cross-alley, and an earlier period; and, as I said before, when seeking it out the other day, there was nothing of it left but the smell. I went up hill and down dale; I inscribed my name in my heart's blood upon jagged masses of brick-work—the said heart's blood being drawn from my shins; I encountered clouds of dust; saw beams, rafters, joists, and laths—slates, tiles, and chimney-pots; saw around me a desolate gaping ruin full of pit-holes and open cellars uniting to trap the unwary. I found the contractors' men, of whom I made inquiry as to this street and that corner, all suffering from the dry limy dust, and also found that their sufferings were augmented by my approach—the poor fellows complaining of being 'choky,' and hinting that there was a public round the corner, just as if you could stand in any street in any town in her Majesty's dominions without finding a "public round the corner."

But even after beer in a gallon-can had made its appearance, there was no sign of Bilger's; and had it not been for the smell, I should not have found out the site, on which like a monument were piled some thousands of bricks.

I knew the smell in a moment. It was a smell never to be forgotten; not the musk, mind, that Mrs. Bilger used to have in penn'orths from chemists for her "hankychy;" but that unmistakable odour of mille-somethings that pervaded Mrs. Bilger's when you passed beneath the portal inscribed " E. Bilger, licensed dealer in tea, coffee, pepper, tobacco, snuff, and vinegar." There was the smell still; and of so lasting a nature, that could Rimmel or Piesse and Lubin condense it, and educate the feminine British to like it, there is a fortune safe.

I leaned one arm upon that brick monument, inhaled the smell, and in a moment I had leaped back years. There I was entering the door, or rather pushing open the little green half gate, whose vicious cracked bell would keep giving tongue so vigorously; there were the little half-hundred sacks of coal which the grimy boy used to take out in the neighbourhood, and which he always called " cools;" there were the halfpenny bundles of wood piled against the counter; the perfume of black puddings; the boxes of bloaters; the bunches of candles—long and short sixes, eights, tens, twelves, and delicate young dips in their teens; Nos. 1, 2, 3, and 4,—portly japanned tin canisters; nests of drawers containing every necessary, from thumb-blue to balls of cotton; toffee in the window, treacly and succulent; soap in bars; tobacco in jars; bacon in slices, and a reserve of a whole half-side; butter in a tub; song-books and sweets on the window-shelves; a pyramid of five Dutch cheeses, and a wedge of single Gloucester on the counter, kept in countenance by a pig-headed bladder of lard, with a greasy knife stuck in what should have been its ear; eggs at eighteen a shilling, enough to have set all the dirty ragged hens that were peeking up and down the dirty alley, while the asthmatic cock with one eye tried once more to finish that crow in which he always broke down half-way, perhaps from modesty. Flies everywhere; salt pork sometimes, fried fish often; and then behind the counter, from first opening in the morning, doing a brisk trade, until last thing at night, Mrs. Bilger, fat and fifty, smiling upon Tot in her high chair.

Who was Tot? What a question! Why, there was not a soul, old or young, from Bell-yard to Clement's-lane and back again, that did not know Bilger's Tot. Pale, sad-faced women looked upon her with brightened eyes; hulking ruffians, seeking " arf-hounce o' backer, missus," looked less gruff in her presence; boys brought her presents of stale pastry, roasted " taters," pease-pudding on paper, and peppermint-stick; or for playthings marbles, suckers, or split tops. Young Rokes, who blacked boots at Temple Bar, had brought her a bad penny he had taken, after a hard struggle with self, for he wanted to nail it upon his box, in company with ten more " duffers," of which he was proud; girls of twelve washed the dirt off one side of their faces on to the other and back again, smeared their hair and foreheads with some of Mrs. Bilger's oil, and then came and made their best curtseys, and " might they take Miss Tot out a bit?" But only seldom was that favour accorded, and not to anyone, be sure; while the incense brought by young worshippers at the shrine was duly sorted, and only accepted as a great honour to the donor.

Not know Tot? Mrs. Bilger's idol, everybody's idol, with her blue eyes and sunny hair, and a little spot here, as if a tiny finger had depressed the soft flesh, and another there; while round the dimples in her chin was a faint flush of the same tint as that in her little cheeks. Not know Tot? Come in with me, and stand aside while a few customers are served; for Tot is learning to talk, and progressing fast.

"Ounce tea, quartern of sugar, and a penny rasher," exclaims one visitor, who, aware of the writing upon the black board overhead, "No trust," has come money in hand, and hammers the counter.

"Ounce tea, twartern," repeats Tot, which is as much of the sentence as she can recollect, when "Bless that bairn!" exclaims Mrs. Bilger, her fat face lighting up, from the mole on what should be the apex of her chin, but is level surface, right up to the black-silk parting of her askew front. And so it is with every customer, Tot taking her lessons in language from real life, and standing a fair chance of picking up a little of the sister-island twang.

But it is tea-time, and the tin kettle is singing upon the narrow hob of the little fire behind the counter, for the back-room is cold and cheerless and dark. There is a rickety round table that just fits in the corner, and its accessories for the meal are all drawn out together from a cupboard, ready spread upon a little black tray, whose black pot receives its due number of spoonfuls from one of the large canisters.

People come in and people go out while Mrs. Bilger and Tot partake of their repast, but that makes no difference; and the toast is begun by Tot and finished by Mrs. Bilger, and then eaten by the old lady with the greatest of gusto, in spite of sundry patches of black and burnings received at the hands of the little girl.

And then ask Mrs. Bilger, and she would tell

you the history of "that child" in whispers; for she was "that sharp, bless you," that nothing could be like it. But this was only Mrs. Bilger's history, and narrators do differ so. Why, the old lady would leave out the acts of one of the principal personages in the little drama; and I had to pick up a bit here from Mrs. Scuffles, who goes out washing, and sift that of the irrelevant matter, and a bit there from Mrs. Molloy, who chars, "God bless you, for a shilling a day and her bit o' meat," though this latter lady's supply possessed very few grains of wheat among the chaff. But the amended history was in this fashion.

Mike had put up the shutters and fastened the cellar-flap, upon one of those dense yellow November nights. It seemed as though the whole of the smoke vomited from London's myriad chimneys was settling down again upon the city; and through every chink, and beneath the door, it crept into Bilger's. It is nothing to say that Cress-alley was dark; it had been dark all day, so that Mrs. Bilger had burned her paraffin-lamp; and now, after carefully trimming it once more, and piling up a few of the nubbly coals that Mike had brought in before he left, and poking an eligible scrap in here between the bars, and just there where there was a glowing spot, sometimes with the tongs and sometimes with her fingers, Mrs. Bilger prepared to make herself comfortable.

Some people might not have thought that behind Mrs. Bilger's counter was a cosy place, but Mrs. Bilger differed, and in spite of the proximity of her stock-in-trade, she was most thoroughly happy there; and now having counted the money out of the till into her pocket, and given a little black saucepan upon the hob a shake, which sent forth a gush of odorous steam, she drew a small black bottle from the cupboard, and set it upon her round table in company with a glass and spoon, while by pulling open a drawer lumps of sugar *ad libitum* could be obtained.

Now when one sees such preparations as these, thoughts will arise of steaming potations; and no doubt Mrs. Bilger would have directly indulged in something of the kind—highly needful, too, upon such a night—had not the fates been adverse; for just as she was seating herself, came from apparently beneath her feet one of the most doleful howls imaginable by anyone who has never heard a cat in distress. Some people may have heard the feline wail; and evidently Mrs. Bilger was familiar with the cry, for she stamped her foot, cried "Ciss!" and exclaimed, "Drat that cat!"

But apparently there was no one at hand to perform the necessary dratting; and though Mrs. Bilger sat down and tried to forget its existence, the cat asserted itself so loudly that Mrs. Bilger was compelled to rise and take down a key from a nail in the edge of a shelf.

"As if that lazy rascal couldn't have seen that there wasn't a cat in the cellar before he locked up," she muttered; and then, unhasping the door, Mrs. Bilger was compelled to open the cellar-flap, descend into the black chasm, and then "ssh" and throw pieces of coal and bundles of wood into dark corners to dislodge the enemy of her peace, the latter articles acting after the manner of built-up shells, and exploding in scattered fragments in the most happy and undoubtedly cat-scaring way; for after a dexterous shy into one corner, there was a crash, a scuffle, the fall of a small avalanche of coals, a rush, and it was evident that the cat was gone; when, hurrying up and banging down the cellar-flap, Mrs. Bilger once more stood inside her shop, and was about closing the door.

"Ha'penny bundle o' wood," said a small voice, and a little active figure suddenly appeared out of the fog.

"Past shop-time," replied Mrs. Bilger, banging the door and rattling up the bar, while out of revenge the imp began to kick at the panel. But he shortly ceased, for it was labour in vain, and Mrs. Bilger commenced solacing herself with something to take the fog out of her throat. Before long, however, came another summons, and another, consisting of kicks at the door, rattlings of the thumb-latch, or metallic taps with a piece of money.

But Mrs. Bilger did not move even when came the tempting sound of coin: she was open from seven in the morning until eight at night, and anyone who came before or after those hours obtained no goods at Bilger's.

An hour passed: the contents of the black saucepan had been discussed, and "just half a glass more" of that warm fluid prepared; the fire burned brightly, and dropped a few cinders with a musical tinkle, while the flames danced and fluttered like golden wings above the ruddy orange caverns in the grate. Mrs. Bilger was thinking of the departed Joseph Bilger, her lord, and his donkey, with which he used to drive a good peripatetic trade in vegetables: the donkey that would go so well on Sundays, when they went out for a drive; the well-bred donkey that fetched three pounds ten, although it had a wretched little bald tail it was so ashamed of that it used to tuck it in between its legs, out of sight, as it trotted along the road. Mrs. Bilger was in a pleasant though sad reverie, when there came another summons at the door, and then what sounded like a moan.

"That 'orrid cat!" muttered Mrs. Bilger; but the knock was repeated again and again, and a voice demanded admittance in so peremptory a manner, that Mrs. Bilger was fain to rise and open the door, though not before she had recognised the voice as that of the policeman on the beat.

"Now then," said the man, "do you know anything of this?"

Mrs. Bilger looked down at "this," to dimly make out that it was a woman's figure; while before she could raise any objection, Z 2999 had lifted the recumbent figure inside the shop.

"Let her be here till I get help," said the policeman; and the next minute Mrs. Bilger found herself holding up the head of her strange visitor, in a confused state of mind as to what she ought to do.

But Mrs. Bilger soon found what she ought to do; for a feeble cry under the shawl of the helpless figure roused her woman's nature, and reminded her of a tiny clay-cold face that she had kissed thirty years before, ere it was hidden from her sight by a little white coffin-lid.

"O, if there was only more room!" she cried, for everything was in her way; but before five minutes were over there was a little carefully-tied-up bundle lying in the warm glow of the fire in an egg-basket; the lamp had been trimmed, and cast down its light upon the pale face and closed eyes of a young girl; and then, before removing the wet shawl and boots, Mrs. Bilger had closed and fastened her door once more, with the determination not to open it until the morning.

And she did not. "Come in the morning!" she shouted to the two policemen who waited outside with their stretcher; and after a little parley, they laughed and went away, to come the next morning and learn that the poor thing was too ill to be moved.

One month, two months, six months did Mrs. Bilger tend the bedside of her strange visitor—a woman upon whose face she had never before gazed, but which possessed that in its wan appealing aspect that made its way to the widow's heart.

"O, them men, them men!" exclaimed Mrs. Bilger, shaking her head fiercely at the doctor. "There's a pretty story here, if we could get to the rights of it."

Mrs. Bilger might have said the wrongs of it; and the mild quiet doctor looked quite uncomfortable, and as if he thought that Mrs. Bilger blamed him. But she did not—only launched her anathemas upon some unknown head; and then to the neglect of her business she nursed the poor, lost, helpless girl, who had sunk down footsore and jaded at her door, worn-out, fever-stricken, abandoned, and desolate, a pariah of our social state. And why? Was it because of her wan helpless face? or was it the feeble cry of the child she held to her heart, which made its way to Mrs. Bilger's breast? Who knows? But let that rest: there, night and day, sat Mrs. Bilger, sobbing bitterly at times to hear the wanderings of the hapless girl, watching the struggle going on for life in that feeble frame, the weary tossing head, and the restless looks from those eyes that were so bright.

Now she would ask eagerly for her child, and when it was brought, sit up in bed and croon over it, hushing it to sleep, weeping and sobbing over it, and calling it by the most endearing terms. The love, the wondrous love of the young mother would be poured forth upon the unconscious babe; and poor Mrs. Bilger would cry silently behind the bed-curtains, and mutter to herself, "O, them men, them men!" as she looked on. Then a change would take place, and, talking hurriedly, the young mother would glance eagerly round the room, seeing no one in her wild mania.

"No one would know, no one would know," she would mutter hoarsely, and holding the little one at arm's length; "no one would know, no one would know! The river—the bridge—the water—no one would know!" And this she would repeat incessantly, giving forth incoherently the thoughts, the dread thoughts, that had haunted her in that sore time of her shame. Shuddering and frightened, Mrs. Bilger would snatch the child from

her arms, in dread lest something more horrible
might befall it; when the mother would wail and
beseech her to bring it back,—now thinking that
the little one had been stolen from her, now that
she had crushed out the feeble flickering flame of
its life.

"Will He be very angry with me—very, very
angry with me?" she would whisper. "I did
not mean to do it, but something made me. O, I
loved it so much—its little soft face, its tiny hands;
and I cried over it again and again; but something made me—something I could not fight with
—and I was obliged; and then I stood on the
bridge, and looked down at the cold black water;
and I was afraid, I was afraid!"

"Cry!" Mrs. Bilger would say. "Could you
have stood by the poor young thing's bedside, and
had her clasping your hands, and flinging her
white arms round your neck, as she begged of you
to give her back her little one—poor daft thing,
taking no notice of it lying in her lap—calling
you 'dear' and 'darling,' and all in a sweet,
gentle, well-bred way; and telling you that if
you'd only give her back her baby, she would go
away and come back no more?

"Poor soul, poor soul! she was going away
then so fast, so fast. She was nothing to me,
nothing at all; but how could I have the heart to
let them take her to the workhouse—she, a poor

child almost, not eighteen, I know. O, them men, them men! I cried, as I never cried before, not even when my own little one was taken, or when poor Joe whispered to me 'Good-bye, Bet; see that Jerry has a good master'—and that was the donkey. O, them men, them men! I'm only a poor, simple, weak woman; but whenever I see all that again, the tears will come pouring down, and I can't keep them back. And I can always see it; for she grew worse and worse till the last, when she was quite quiet, and lay there with little Tot pressed close to her, and her eyes wide open, as if she was trying to make out what it all meant, for she had never been sensible before. I went in and out gently; but the eyes still kept following me about, and, as I thought, looked anxious, till I went close up to her side, and she tried to lift her poor white hand, but it fell again. Then she looked at me, and then at the little one, as was sleeping so calm and innocent by her side; and as her lips moved I leaned over, and just caught the one word, ' Baby!' just like as if it was breathed.

"Ah, poor soul, poor soul! she was sensible then for the first time, though she didn't know me, or what it all meant; but I understood her, and I felt something was coming, and fell upon my knees by the bed, sobbing out, 'God bless it, I will!' And then, through my dim eyes, I seemed to see her give me one look, and smile like at me; and then I jumped up again, feeling half mad, and lifted the baby and held it to her, when her lips formed themselves as if to kiss its little cheek; while then I couldn't see any more for crying.

"Gone?—yes, she was gone, as she said, never to come back no more; and I said I would take care of it, and I have.—And whose darling are you, Tot?" exclaimed the stout, homely old woman.

"Gan'ma's," said the little thing, looking sidewise at the stranger.

But Bilger's is gone, and the brick heap monument stands in its place. I stand there too, picturing again the homely shop, the homely face of the owner; and her words yet ring in my ear as I think of the gentle, God-implanted love in that simple woman's breast; and then I turn away, thinking of the moral of her sad story.

I believe I said that Mrs. Bilger now lived at Hanwell. Some people said it was the best place for her.

A Christmas Fairy.

BY HENRY J. BYRON.

I.

Only a Fairy for Christmas-time—
    Just for the month, or the two months, say;
Nothing approaching the true sublime
    Regular genuine tricksy fay;
Only a fairy by name indeed,
    Just while her gauze and her tinselled dress
Cover her poor little limbs: agreed;
    Say—would you wish to know further? Yes?

II.

Only a Fairy for just to-night,
    Dull little drudge with the dawn of day;
Out of the beautiful pale lime-light,
    Merely a thin little girl in gray.
Small and shabby, and scantly fed,
    Born to toil and a life of care,
Waking up when it's time for bed—
    Big-eyed baby with golden hair.

Gustave Doré, del.	Dalziel Bros., sc.

CENDRILLON.

III.

Follow her home when her night-work's done;
    Trudging wearily back she goes,
Back to bed about half-past one;
    Terrible hour to seek repose!
Most little children so long in bed,
    Sleeping peacefully, but my fay
Seeks her mean little couch instead
    At the glimmer of coming day.

IV.

Wearily sleeping, but dreaming too—
    Dreaming mayhap she may one day be
Dressed like that beautiful nymph in blue
    Who's so tremendous a salary.
Think of the joy on the Saturday,
    Taking that glorious sum to those—
Those who look on her paltry pay
    As something meaning both food and clothes.

V.

Cheery her voice in that dismal room,
    Sun-bright face with a smile that warms;
Lightsome her laugh in the midst of gloom,
    Small home-fairy whose presence charms—
Charms with mysterious strange delight;
    So all the neighbours agree and say,
" Surely this golden-haired, elfish sprite,
    Fairy at *night*, is the same by *day*."

Characters and Scenes.

By Edward Draper.

FIVE-AND-THIRTY years ago London-bred boys scarcely spent their time so pleasantly as their successors do now. Let us begin with the matter of costume. Without the aid of a pencil it would be difficult to indicate to the present youthful generation the absurd appearance presented by a boy in the full-dress of—let us say 1830. Here is a sketch which may answer the purpose.

It will be at once evident, that every article of this wretched child's attire is constructed with a view to his personal misery. Note well that ridiculous cap, with its circumference of cane, which, protruding, in fulness of time, will be drawn out to serve for purposes of castigation. Observe the Panjandrum button at the top, to which is affixed a silken braid, whence dangles a foolish tassel, which, inevitably attaining the miserable urchin's mouth, will give him experience of the flavour of silk and dye for the remainder of his days. Mark

the exasperating japanned-leather chin-strap; also
the maddening collar pinned in front. This latter will be constantly coming unfastened, and will
then exhibit some half-yard of cambric, edged
with an idiotic frill, streaming down his back. His
skeleton suit of short-waisted jacket and thin " nan-
keens," buttoned outside, is purposely so contrived

that he can only by dint of great trouble get into
it or out of it. His shoes are tied with ribbons.
Only fancy a parent calmly contemplating a big
boy of his own with shoe-ties, and entertaining no
sense of the absurd therein!

This poor boy was unhappy at school. *Nicho-
las Nickleby* had not as yet exploded the brutal-

ity of the pedagogue; and the scholastic system
was of the simplest. The pupil's lessons were set
him, and he was thrashed whenever unable to repeat them *verbatim*, without reference to his com-
prehension. He was indeed thrashed for every
thing, from spilling a blot of ink to breaking a
window. Sometimes a boy was thrashed simply
for not having been thrashed. So it was with
Jonkins. He was a very good boy, who learnt
all his lessons, never blotted his copy-book, did all
his sums, called out the names of his schoolfellows
when they tried to talk in school-hours; never
fought, and was the greatest sneak in the school.
One day he was thus accosted by a big fellow:
"Jonkins, you haven't been caned for some time.
I think a hiding would do you good." He had
it; and the aggressor was thrashed in his turn by
the master.

But the London boy, as if to console him for
his many miseries, had one source of supreme enjoyment. This was his theatre. The stage sometimes relieved even his school torments. One of
his daily reading-lessons was usually taken from
the drama, and at the Christmas breaking-up it
was not at all unusual for the boys to play regular
set pieces, with accessories of scenery and costume.
An abridged version of *Richard the Third*, the
scene between Arthur and Hubert in *King John*,
and the farce of *Turning the Tables*, were in great

favour on such occasions. Moreover, nearly every boy had a toy-theatre, with its pasteboard characters and scenes, either his own, or joint property of himself and his "partner."

These "characters and scenes" must by no means be judged of by the wretched little sheets still occasionally exhibited in the windows of sweet-stuff shops in metropolitan alleys. In those days they were really artistic pictures. The chief publisher was one West, who kept a shop opposite the Olympic Theatre in Wych-street. His colouring was quite a marvel of effectiveness. The scenes were engraved by clever scene-painters, who designed and carried out many of the originals under the tasteful management of Madame Vestris, at the theatre across the road. The characters were etched by skilful artists, and were so well drawn that they frequently presented actual portraits of the performers. Karl, for instance, in the *Miller and his Men*, is still easily to be recognised as Liston; and the likeness is carried on throughout the various positions of the character. I have mentioned the colouring; it was often the work of the late William Heath, famous in his day as a water-colour painter and etcher. His caricatures and plates of military costume are still well remembered. There are yet extant entire sets of characters and scenes painted by the late celebrated John Varley, and by Alfred Cocking, the unfortunate artist who sacrificed his life to a craze about a novel form of parachute.

When the long evenings rendered out-door amusements impossible, the toy-theatre was the one absorbing delight of the boys; and very frequently of their fathers. To carry out a play, from the preliminary saving of the pocket-money to the purchase or construction of the theatre, the colouring, pasting down, and cutting out of the characters, and the final fruition in a state performance on the parlour-table before an admiring party, was something really worthy of a boy's ambition. It had, moreover, the beneficial effect, beyond the mere exercise of ingenuity and industry, of practically familiarising him with form and colour. Probably many an artist of the present day first conceived a love for art from being taught the use of his colour-box upon characters and scenes. It is true, there were certain difficulties inseparable from a dramatic performance carried on through the medium of pasteboard. In whatever attitude a character entered, he remained unalterable until his "exit," and when, as not unfrequently happened, he fell upon his face, he became instantly invisible except as an edge. But these small drawbacks only served to stimulate imagination.

An artist, now renowned as a sculptor and illustrator, perfected, when a lad, a wonderful representation of the *Miller and his Men*. The scenes were painted and the characters coloured, cut out, and spangled in a style of unparalleled magnificence. A grand performance was announced, and so great was the renown of the *mise-en-scène*, that a large audience of boys, at a penny per head, was collected in a corn-loft belonging to the father of the projector. Gunpowder and red fire were liberally provided to give effect to the explosion at the *finale*, stage-lamps were dangerously plentiful, and the performance proceeded with great *éclat* until a disaster occurred in the middle of the second act. The manager's papa, armed with a horsewhip, suddenly appeared above the ladder, and the catastrophe was supplied by a liberal thrashing bestowed with like goodwill upon the management and what actors call " the front of the house."

It may be wondered how an amusement so popular and so pleasing as the toy-theatre ever fell into decay. It was for this reason: certain speculative print-publishers suddenly filled the market with inferior productions at half the prices previously charged. The boys bought eagerly at first, but soon their instinctive tastes revolted at the miserable substitutes, while the original pictures seemed too dear. But the legitimate trade had been ruined. No boy of ordinary perception would now care to possess the wretched pictures supplied for the toy-stage. The boys, too, seem to have lost, with their toy, the relish for dramatic entertainments. One now seldom sees a young fellow at the play, unless indeed at a broad burlesque. You may talk to a score before you can find one who can quote half a dozen lines of Shakespeare, or handle his pencils. Instead of the intellectual pleasures of the theatre, they resort to the less intellectual amusements of the music-hall.

Of course no one would pretend to hold forth the *Miller and his Men* as a highly intellectual play. The alphabet and spelling-book are not great works of literature, but they in like manner are means to an end.

It is now many years since poor West—the great publisher, if not the originator, of characters and scenes—finally closed his little dark shop, whence had emanated so much salutary amusement to the boys of a former age. A short time before his death he commenced selling off all his stock at ridiculously low prices. The poor old man could be heard gasping behind the simple screen which divided his death-bed from the public portion of his shop. There might then be had, capitally drawn, and when coloured, gorgeous as summer flowers, engraved character-portraits of all the dramatic celebrities of a past generation; and these—we allude to the larger prints—were really good characteristic portraits; not, as now, mere outrageous idealised figures sprawled into impos-

"THE LAST ROSE OF SUMMER."

sible attitudes to fill all four corners of the sheet.
The bright colouring of such series as *Blue Beard*,
the *Elephant of Siam*, and the other Oriental plays,
was specially wonderful. The "scenery" was un-
rivalled in its touch and picturesqueness. There
were characters in the *Wild Boy* in which the free
flowing lines of George Cruikshank could easily be
traced, while those in *Tom and Jerry* were etched
by Robert Cruikshank, who partially illustrated the
original work. There were first-proofs coloured by
the artist to guide the ordinary print colourer; and
some of these were as brilliant as though the pencil
of Heath had but just quitted them. The means
by which the extraordinary brightness of West's
colouring was obtained was a continual puzzle to
the boys. Much was certainly due to daring ap-
position of colours; but, even granting this, there
must have been some trade-secret in the prepara-
tion of the pigments. Shortly before West's death,
the late Mr. Albert Smith, happening to pass along
Wych-street, entered the shop and purchased a
copy of every print then remaining on sale.

All the plates are now destroyed, and scarcely
a character, scene, or theatrical portrait of West's
exists save in the folios of collectors. The miserable prints now published in their place are, as
works of art or interest, simply beneath notice.

A Visit

TO THE

PRESIDENT OF THE EARLY-RISING ASSOCIATION.

By George Grossmith.

NE morning I received the following letter from a quiet little town in Milkshire:

"Dear Sir,—The Committee of our Literary Institution have deputed me to request your attendance here to deliver a lecture.

"Speaking individually, I should prefer a *serious* subject; but on behalf of the directors collectively I am bound to say that the writings of Charles Dickens have been mentioned.

"For my own part, I do not like Dickens, never having read his works. Indeed, I consider his repeated attacks on the medical profession (to which I have the honour to belong) most unjust and uncalled-for.

"I have been in the habit of lecturing to our people myself for many years, but I fear my subjects are beyond their grasp; at any rate they seem to require a change.

"I may add that I am also President of the Early-Rising Association in this town. If, therefore, you can introduce anything in your lecture illustrative of the advantages of early rising, you will confer a particular favour on me individually and the committee collectively.

"P.S. There will be a bed in my house at your service, and the first up-train to London leaves here at six o'clock in the morning."

Now I am *not* one of those ingenious professors who undertake to decipher human character through the medium of a person's handwriting and thirteen postage-stamps; but there really was something about the style of this application that enabled me to form an estimate of the writer which proved to be strictly correct in all respects, except that he had a wooden leg, which certainly nothing in the letter had led me to expect.

On my arrival in the town, I sought information as to the whereabouts of my intended host. I was cautioned as to his being a "little eccentric," and warned not to be put out by his peculiarities ; as, apart from these, he was a very worthy and much-respected gentleman.

For example, it was suggested to me that he was in the habit of rising each evening after the lecture to correct any false impressions which the lecturer might have left upon the minds of the people.

Luckily I was spared this humiliation, as I did not happen to touch upon any controversial topics. I seldom do. It doesn't pay, as a rule. But I have encountered a good many "eccentric people" in my wanderings, and mean some day to write a book about them. Once, in Dampshire, the president of a society, sitting just by my side, kept up a running commentary upon my lecture, thus : " Ah, just so !" " Well, very possible." " No, really, you must excuse me *there ;* that won't do down here ; you'd better try that somewhere else." " Very good—ha, ha !" (a horse-laugh). " *I've heard that before.*" And when, at the close of the lecture, I asked how that sort of thing was *tolerated down there*, I was told, with undisguised astonishment at my metropolitan audacity, that the eccentric gentleman was the deputy-lieutenant of the county, and gave the institute twenty pounds a year ! And certainly some of the Mechanics' Institutes in the country would allow any amount of eccentricity at that price.

On another occasion, in Baconshire, I had the misfortune to incur the animosity of an eccentric lady. It was in one of those little country towns where they don't often have lectures, but where, oddly enough, whenever they have *one*, they are pretty certain to have *two* the same night; for, being about equally divided by religious and political differences, such is the neighbourly, friendly spirit in which all matters are conducted there, that whenever one side invites a lecturer down from London, the other section are sure to have one down the same night in opposition. Now I was engaged to hold forth on the *Sketches by Boz*. My rival, in the opposition room, lectured on the *Pilgrim's Progress*. The lady in question—elderly, very respectable, but not very intelligent—wandered from her peaceful home with the view of attending the latter; but she went to the wrong room, and taking her place on the front seat, and putting on the most solemn countenance it was ever my misfortune to behold, became a listener to my discourse on the writings of Boz, and I am certain, for the first twenty minutes, did not discover the mistake she had made. But, alas, when I at length referred to my author's description of a country fair, and the servant-girls out for the day, " not allowed to have any followers at home, but now resolved to have 'em all at once," the dear old soul gave a shriek of horror, and said, quite audibly, "O, how shocking!" This exclamation was repeated when I described "the fat old lady with the Jack-in-the-box, and three shies a penny;" and at last I became somewhat unnerved. I tried not to look at the old lady; but there is nothing in creation more difficult than the effort *not* to look at a thing you don't want to see. At length I approached, with horror, the author's description of a thimble-rig, knowing it would upset her. "Here's a little game to make you wake up and laugh six months after you're dead, buried, and forgotten, and turn the hair of your head gray with delight. Here's three little thimbles and one little pea. Keep your eye on the pea, and never say die! Now then, with a one, two, three, and a three, two, one!" &c. &c. This was quite enough. The old lady, mistaking me for the creature I was describing, and believing that I was offering to bet with the company, uttered a scream of horror and left the room. "Poor lady," said I to the quiet old chairman, "of course she's mad; but why did the committee let her in?" "No, sir," said the president, "that lady is not mad; *she is my wife!*" I apologised; but, to my comfort, the chairman was not so much offended as I supposed; for, addressing me again, he said, "Never mind; you'd better get on with your lecture. *She's more trouble to me than she is to you.* You'd better get on with your lecture."

Recently, an eccentric "secretary," inviting me to lecture for his society, obligingly assured me that he was *not at all particular as to time,* and added, " but please to avoid Advent, Lent, and Passion-week, and we *must* have a market-day and a moonlight night!" while only last week an eccentric clergyman, living within range of the Crystal Palace, objected to my giving readings from *Pickwick* in the parish school-room, to the Working-Man's Institute, on a *Saturday* night, on the ground that " *it was too near Sunday*" *!*

But to return to my friend, the President of the Early-Rising Association.

Having found out his quiet abode, and taken my seat at his table, I soon had an opportunity of studying the peculiar bent of his " eccentricity."

A tall, fine, handsome old gentleman, speaking with a sort of subdued inward voice, and having a strange habit of repeating the last word or two or syllable of each sentence. Thus he addressed me :

"I understand, Mr. Smithers—Mr. Smithers —that you have something to do with *The Thames* newspaper—newspaper; and it has occurred to me—to me—that you might possibly know the editor—the editor. Now within the last two years—two years—I have written as many as forty-seven letters—forty-seven letters—to the editor of that paper—paper—upon questions of medical jurisprudence—prudence; and strange to say, sir—say, sir—not one of those letters has ever been inserted—inserted."

I said I was sorry to hear that.

"Precisely so, sir—so, sir; and if you know the editor—editor—I thought you might not object to ask him—ask him—if he is ever likely to use any of those communications—cations; and, if not, will he kindly return me the letters (for I did not keep copies of them—copies of them) dated the 3d of January last, February the 6th and 12th, March the 19th, and April the 1st—the 1st."

I informed him of the well-known fact that the editor of *The Thames* received daily a sufficient number of letters to occupy the entire space at his disposal; and having satisfied him, I hoped, that it was want of room, and not want of appreciation of his very learned effusions, which had led to their rejection, I was obliged in common honesty to add that there was not the smallest possibility of his ever recovering possession of any document once committed to the charge of Squinting-house-square.

Precisely as the clock struck ten that night, the few guests invited to assemble after the early lecture rose from the supper-table simultaneously, without finishing the conversation in hand, and quietly departed. In a few more minutes my eccentric host placed a chamber-candlestick in my hands, and said that he would show me to my room. I rose and followed the wooden leg upstairs. He then told me that he would call and fetch my candle in ten minutes. I said I would blow it out; but as this intimation did not appear to satisfy him, and I heard the wooden leg hovering about impatiently on the landing, I extinguished the "flaming minister" and jumped into bed.

About seven minutes afterwards, as it seemed to me (although, I confess, on reference to my watch, I find it to be as many hours), I heard that wooden leg again on the stairs. It entered my room, lit up my candle with a wax taper, said it was "past five o'clock—o'clock," and walked out again.

I regarded this as a strong hint that I must get up; and while I was endeavouring to realise the suggestion in my mind, I must have dozed off; for I was again disturbed from a half-broken reverie by the noise of that wooden leg on the stairs. It entered my room, went straight up to the candle, snuffed it sharply, said nothing, and went out again.

I saw that but one course was open to me; and while struggling manfully with the temptation to defer it, I again dropped off—travelled about 400 miles, lectured to 3000 people, supped with the president, heard his daughters sing and play delightfully, broke down in a comic song myself, and was being precipitated, with thirteen railway-carriages, from a Cornish viaduct 1200 feet high (all in five minutes)—when, for the *third* time, I heard the sound of that terrible wooden leg on the stairs. In a moment I was out of bed. My first impulse was to rush to the candle and snuff it. I then knocked over two chairs, to satisfy my host of my rapid progress in dressing; and, hastening downstairs (all thought of shaving with the cold hot water on the table being out of the question), I stumbled out an abject apology—" hoped I had not kept him waiting," &c. &c. With characteristic candour he replied that I had, but that " it was of no consequence, except that the coffee was quite cold—quite cold," and " the *first up-train to London had gone.*"

I left my eccentric friend shortly afterwards with the melancholy conviction that I had lost caste for ever, as no doubt I had done, in the estimation of the " President of the Early-Rising Association."

E. Hull, del.　　　　　Dalziel Bros., sc.

LOVE'S SEASONS.

Harrison Weir, del. Dalziel Bros., sc.

FAITHFUL UNTO DEATH.

DEALINGS WITH THE DEVIL.

By H. Sutherland Edwards.

"A dark and stormy demon hovered over the bottomless pit, when above him shone a bright and beautiful angel. The spirit of denial, the spirit of doubt, saw the sweet vision and shed a tear of compunction. I have seen thee, thou bright one, and thou shon'st not on me for nothing! Not all in the heaven I hated, not all in the earth I despised!"
Pushkin.

PLAYGOERS must have observed that no class of pieces are so uniformly successful as those in which the devil, or diabolical agency, or a personage possessing diabolical attributes, is introduced. If no devil nor imp in any shape can be brought in, it is sometimes enough to pay the fiend the compliment of recognition by mentioning him in the title—as, for instance, in *Fra Diavolo*. In support of the general proposition, *Don Juan*, *Faust*, *Der Freischütz*, *Robert le Diable*, the *Devil on two Sticks*, the *Devil to Pay*, and a long list of favourite works, including three or four masterpieces, might be pointed to. Recourse to the devil's aid may be had in various ways; but when a diabolical atmosphere pervades the whole play, as in *Der Freischütz*, it is not found necessary to do homage to the evil spirit in the playbill; nor when his name is made so conspicuous and is repeated so often as it is in *Fra Diavolo*, does it seem requisite that he or his should be mixed up with the action of the drama. Let the least acknowledgment of his power in any shape be made, and the Prince of Darkness, who is notoriously a gentleman, is sure to respond.

It is true that in *Faust*, *Der Freischütz*, *Robert*, and most works in which a struggle between the principles of good and evil is exhibited, the devil in the end generally comes off second-best. Still, there he is. Instead of being ignored, as practically he is in modern everyday life, he is caused to figure as an important and irresistible agent in human affairs, and only succumbs at last to that higher Power, beneath whose blows even the Napoleon imagined by Victor Hugo fell crushed at Waterloo. Besides, how many people wait to see the *dénouement* of these pieces? *Robert le Diable* is a magnificent opera, but it is in five acts; and if everyone does not leave the theatre after the trio in the fifth, even the few who remain begin to think of going; and the final overthrow of the satanic Bertram is scarcely witnessed by anyone. One can fancy the arch-fiend saying to himself, with a diabolical grin : " M. Meyerbeer wishes me to be beaten in the end, does he! Let him compose his opera in five acts, and no one will stay to see whether I am beaten or not."

Everyone, we should think, must wait for the last piece in *Der Freischütz ;* but here, though the satanic character undoubtedly gets the worst of it, he is shamefully cheated, so that a certain amount of sympathy is felt for him by all justminded spectators.

But in every literary work in which the hero makes a formal compact with the fiend, diabolical interests are, on the whole, very well served ; and this from the time of Theophilus of Syracuse,* the first man who is recorded to have formally sold himself to the devil, though by no means the first, and certainly not the last, who has done so unformally, perhaps even unconsciously, but actually all the same. In all these cases it is a decided advantage to the hero to have bartered away his soul, as *per* agreement. He invariably gets it back again in the end, and in the mean time he is all-powerful in worldly matters. No woman can resist his eyes, nor can any man stand against his sword. Every wish that he may form, while the

---

* His interesting history has been written by Dr. G. W. Dasent, and is published at Messrs. Pickering's.

compact lasts, is gratified; and finally, when he wants to cheat the devil, all he has to do is to repent for five minutes and be eternally saved. This is not a bad career; and it is pretty nearly the career of Faust, as the drama, whether in a purely dramatic or in an operatic form, is represented on our stage; of Robert, in Meyerbeer's celebrated work; and of Rodolph, in *Der Freischütz*.

Don Juan, who has come to no regular understanding with the fiend, does not escape so easily; and this shows the disadvantage of not conducting your affairs, whatever they may be, in a proper business-like manner. Don Juan has opened an account with the infernal regions, but without seeing the head of the establishment, and without making any arrangement as to when and where he is to pay. It seems to have been the usual practice at this shop to make customers enter into personal recognisances beforehand; and as their agreements and bonds were always proved to be worthless when payment was demanded, all who conformed to the rules of the establishment got off scot-free. Don Juan, however, was too lawless even for the infernal regions. Otherwise the eternally devoted Elvira might have saved him, through the artful device of shifting his responsibility on to some other and more unfortunate man.

That stories of diabolical agency have a great charm for the public cannot be denied; it may be argued, however, that it is not because the agency is diabolical, but simply because it is supernatural, that they are found so fascinating. Oddly enough, though the devil is allowed to work his worst on our stage, it may be doubted whether the exhibition of supernatural agency of a heavenly origin would be tolerated in England. When *Robert le Diable* was first produced in London, it excited a perfect storm of disapprobation; and "shocking," "revolting," were the mildest epithets applied to it. Since then, however, the devil has become a perfectly well-received personage at English theatres. We didn't like him at first, but we have become used to him, as we get used to other bad things; and the introduction of Satan himself on the stage would now cause very little astonishment. After all, the devil never swears; so that he is a much less objectionable character, as far as his language is concerned, than many of our low comedians.

But even in France, where nothing seems to be thought too sacred or too profane for stage-representation, it may be doubted whether the *holy supernatural* could be introduced with any great success. There is no piquancy about a miracle performed by legitimate means. Thus the miracle of the roses, in the beautiful legend of Elizabeth of Hungary, produces but little effect in the dramatised version of the story, as given on the French stage. "Progress," in dramatic affairs has taken a strange direction. We began with mystery-plays and moralities based on sacred subjects. At present we banish sacred subjects absolutely from the theatre, and give all the best dramatic situations, as it has been said that we give all the best tunes, to the devil.

Yet there is one charming story of the supernatural, hitherto undramatised, which possesses points in common with each of the three legends of Theophilus, of Faust, and of Don Juan, and in which the triumph of the good over the bad is not a sort of after-thought tacked on to the play like an epilogue, but an essential part of the drama. Let us finish our "Dealings with the Devil" by giving a short account of the only man of whom we can find it recorded that, having once put himself in communication with the evil spirit, he had yet sufficient strength left to refuse the terms proposed to him, and to break off the negotiations.

In one of a collection of *Contes Dévots* belonging to the twelfth century, it is narrated that a certain nobleman being unable to touch the heart of a fair lady whom he loved, "and whom he even wished to marry," lost his appetite and took an aversion to life. In this condition he heard of a Jew, a great astrologer and necromancer, to whose occult science he was urged to have recourse. He began by making the magician a handsome present, after which he told him the story of his unrequited love, and offered him an immense sum of money if he would enable him to gain the affection of the beautiful lady.

The Jew said it was the easiest thing in the world; but that in the first place the nobleman must renounce " God, the saints, and the holy Virgin."

" No," said the nobleman, who understood the art of selling himself to the devil, and wished to secure a means of escape from his compact, " anything else you please, but not the Virgin."

" A virgin, more or less, in an affair of this kind is not important," observed the Jew.

" I refuse positively to renounce the holy Virgin," persisted the nobleman.

The Jew understanding how, if he acceded to the nobleman's views, the whole bargain might easily be rendered null and void,* declined to do business, and the nobleman went away in despair.

On his road home he entered a church, threw himself on his knees before an image of the holy Virgin, to show he was faithful above all things,

* It was by the direct aid of the holy Virgin that Theophilus of Syracuse got himself set free from the terms of his bond.

and implored her help, praying either that he might obtain the lady of his heart, or that he might cease to love her.

His prayer was granted, in token of which the Virgin bowed her head. But he was so full of his love and so intent on his devotions, that he did not see the sign, and continued kneeling and praying.

The lady of his heart, however, had been all this time in the church, and had noted the Virgin's gracious action; and she understood that this Christian man was loved by the holy Mary, and that she ought to love him also. Accordingly, she followed him when he left the church, and asked him why his face was so changed, and where he had been since she had last seen him. He answered, by telling her all that he had done since she had refused him, and what his prayers had been to St. Mary.

"St. Mary has rewarded you for your devotion to her," replied the lady, "for I will be your wife whenever you please."

George Cruikshank, del.　　　　　　　　Dalziel Bros., sc.

BETWEEN THE TRAINS.

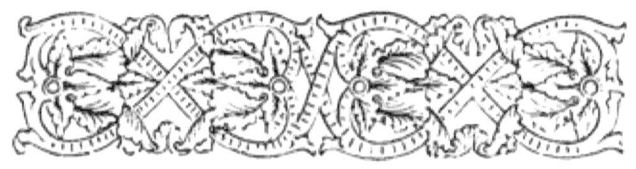

A Scrap from a Comedy.*

BY DION BOUCICAULT.

---o---

Scene—*A Bedchamber.*

Nettletop *in bed, shamming sick. He has been divorced by his wife* Isabella, *but still is in love with her. He desires to attract her sympathy and play upon her feelings by spreading a report that he is at death's-door.*

Enter Dr. Minimum.

Nettletop. Ah, Dr. Minimum, how good of you to come so promptly!

Minimum. No worse symptoms, I hope, sir?

Nettle. The heart, doctor; the heart.

Min. Allow me to feel your pulse. Ah!—um!—no fever there. How is it with the appetite?

Nettle. I live on smoke and alcohol chiefly.

Min. The absence of fever, in presence of such products of irritation, is a curious feature—very curious. In what form do you exhibit alcohol?

Nettle. In the shape of brandy and soda.

* From *How she loves him.*

Min. Ha!— of course — of course! Internal fever, conquered by a febrile stimulant — *similia similibus!* Yours is a most interesting case, and one in which the allopathic treatment exhibits its deficiency in a singular manner. Large doses of physic, sir, would only irritate you.

Nettle. They always d-d-did.

Min. It is the homœopathic practice to explain to the patient the pathology of his disorder, so that he may feel an interest in his progress, and accompany his own case.

Nettle. Be introduced—into himself, as it were; be t-t-taken in.

Min. Precisely. The seat of your complaint is in the sternum.

Nettle. (*sitting up*). You astonish me!

Min. Here it lies; the anterior of the thorax in its median line. Your diagnosis portends a morbid inflammation of the pectoralis major, pleuritis muscularis. Take in a deep breath; ah—so, that pains you?

Nettle. (*lies down*). N-n-not in the least.

Min. (*disconcerted*). Ah!—um!—a bad sign, sir; an insidious indication when nature won't do what she ought. (*Taking out a case.*) You have water here? So the pectoralis major is evidently in sympathy with some more important organ, which we must make to speak. We will exhibit aconite in alternation with belladonna; then we shall try pulsatilla (*Minimum prepares doses in two tumblers*).

Nettle. You could not give me a little of Isabella, could you? (*Sitting up.*)

Min. You have no fever. We must create some. Every disease is its own antidote.

Nettle. Just as marriage is the cure for love.

Min. Nature is full of corroborating evidence. Three drops in a pint of water—one teaspoonful every Wednesday night. You will commence with No. 1. If not attended with relief, we'll try something else, and so go on changing till you are cured. The old system would have attacked your disorder with a prescription; that is, sixteen homicidal drugs compounded into one conspiracy against your inside. Now we explore the mystery with one agent at a time, trying the whole pharmacopœia without prejudice, until the patient is well; the last dose proving that we have hit on the remedy required.

Nettle. And if he die?

Min. I can defy our worst enemies to say we killed him.

Nettle. Doctor, I feel better already.

Min. That's faith, sir. Faith, sir, is the only medicine which homœopathy permits to be taken in allopathic doses. Good-morning—good-morning.

BILL BANKS'S DAY OUT.

BY THE JOURNEYMAN ENGINEER,
Author of "Some Habits and Customs of the Working Classes."

O you know what I've been thinking, Bill?" said my Bessie to me the other evening, almost before I could get inside the door.

"Well, about getting me something nice for tea, I hope," I says, for I had been out with goods from before four o'clock in the morning, and was precious hungry.

"Yes, I've thought of that," she says, nodding towards a couple of nice bloaters, bristling before the fire; "but that wasn't exactly what I meant."

"Why, then, my dear," I says, beginning to slip into my tea, "if what you did mean ain't *very* particular, and it's all the same to you, suppose you let me finish my tea and have a wash before you tell me what it is?"

"Well, I can do that, Bill," she says; "but you needn't have been so snappy about it."

"If I *was* snappy, Bessie," I says, "you must blame it on the hunger; for you'll see that when he's polished off the herrings, and this plate of toast, and got the regulation three cups of 'best mixed' into him, your William will be his good-humoured self again.

"And now, Bessie my lass," I says, when, after having a wash and putting off my greasy overalls, I was comfortably seated on my own side of the fireplace, "what have you been thinking about?"

"Well, I know you'll laugh, Bill," she says; "but this afternoon, while I was looking at the book as you've got from the institution, it struck me all of a minute, why shouldn't our Bill write something for print? he's a good scholard, better than most working men, and he's read no end of books."

"Don't talk silly," I says; "what could I write about?"

"O, thank you for the compliment," says she; "but I didn't know as how I *was* talking silly; and as to what you'd write about, why there's lots of things."

"Well, never mind the lots," I says, "just let's hear you name one, and then perhaps I'll talk to you."

"Why," she says, thinking for a minute, "you could write about when we went Saint-Mondaying to Hampton Court awhile back. Other people are always writing about their holidays, and I don't see why a working man shouldn't write about his; he earns 'em hard enough, and has few enough on 'em, goodness knows."

"Well, that's right enough as far as it goes, Bessie," I says, "and I would write in a minute, only, don't you see, very little of that sort of thing's two penn'orth, and it's guineas to gooseberries against getting it printed."

"O, I can't see that," says Bessie; "a holiday is a holiday all the world over, and if editors, as they call 'em, 'll print about one holiday, surely they will about another, or else they must be curious characters."

"Well," I says, "if any of them was to hear you going on in that style, they would think *you* was a curious character, anyway."

"O, you needn't get on with your sneering to me, Bill," she says, quite huffed; "I daresay I could talk to a gentleman quite as well as you; and there's some of these 'ere editors as are no great shakes, after all; for how anyone calling himself a scholard, and pretending to know what's what, could put such rubbish into his paper as them what-you-may-call-'em articles—well, leading articles, you knew very well what I meant—as that fool of a Dick Barnes comes here reading to you of a night, gets over me. He's a pretty character to have coming after you, *he is*. Tries

to come the grand over everybody, just because
his wife's aunt left him them four rickety old
houses, as he'll have drunk away before another
year's over his head, if he goes on as he's been
doing lately. I don't know how you can have the
patience to sit there listening to him; and I just
tell you what it is,—I ain't going to have him a-
coming here any more asking me to go for his
dirty pots of four-ale and screws of tobacco; and
getting on with his rights of property—pretty property *his* is to brag about!—and suchlike nonsense,
till one can't hear their own ears; and if you
don't send him packing the next time he comes
here a-spitting on the fire-irons, and making a
pot-house of my clean kitchen, I *will*, and with a
flea in his ear too; and so mind, I tell you."

"Take wind, my dear," I says, "and give us
the end of my nose back, anyway."

"Now you're not going to get my temper out,
Bill," she answers, "and so you needn't try; all
that I've got to say is, that if that drunken, blather-
ing Dick Barnes was to come and ask you to
write something for him, you'd do it in a minute,
for all you're so ready with your excuses when I
want you to oblige me; but never mind, I'll serve
you out for it yet."

"Well, well," says I, "anything for a quiet
life; hand us the writing tackle and the dictionary,
and here goes to do my best, hit or miss."

"Ah, now that's something like!" she says, brightening up in an instant, and reaching the things off the bookshelf; "you know I'd do as much for you any day, now don't you, Bill?"

"I am sure you would, Bessie," I says.

"Yes, that I would!" she says, leaning over my shoulder as I was beginning to write, "and more too if I could. It was the thought of that Dick Barnes coming here drinking, and getting on with his 'representation of real estates,' and all the rest of it—as he knows as much about as a pig does about its grandmother—that put me out of the way just now. However," she finishes, feeling me beginning to wriggle my shoulder, "I'll leave you to it, for my chatter would only hinder you; and so I'll just give Mrs. Jones a call; she's got something particular to tell me about them lot as made a moonlight flit of it from opposite her."

And as it's along of Bessie that this is wrote, so it was along of her that we had the holiday.

"Bill," she says to me, when we were at dinner the Wednesday before, "you ain't been looking over-well this last two or three weeks."

"Ain't I?" I says; "well, I feel well enough, and you can see by the style I'm performing in now, I ain't off my feed any."

"Well, I don't mean to say you look regular ill like," she says, "but you seem fagged, and look as if a bit of a holiday would do you good."

O, O, thinks I, tumbling to her little game in a minute, *that's* the way the bull runs, is it? But I said nothing, and after waiting a bit she went on.

"And so I've been thinking that if we were to have a day out together next Monday, it would freshen you up a bit, and do me no harm. What do you say?"

"Well," I says, "I like a holiday as well as here or there one, but at the same time I think it's only those who can afford holidays who ought to take them; and as times are hard and money not over plentiful, I don't think we can afford one just now."

"O, that's always your tale," says Bessie, firing up in a moment; "we can't afford this and we can't afford that. Bother the afford! We afforded a day out last year, and I don't know as we're any the worse off for it now; and if we afford another, I daresay we won't be any the poorer for it this time next year; and at any rate, it will be all the same in a hundred years to come. Upon my word, Bill," she went on, softening down a bit, "it isn't nice of you. You know, though I say it as shouldn't, I'm as good a manager as most, and never waste a penny; and it ain't what I expected of you, to begin about 'can't afford it,' as if I was some waster, when I asked you to have a day out, and for your own good too!"

Well, I saw she meant to have her own way,

and I thought I might as well knock under first as last, and so I says, "I know you mean well, Bessie, and we *will* have a holiday; for, after all, it's a poor heart that never rejoices, and as the song says, if we mean to go it, let's go it while we're young."

"Ay, that's yer sort, Bill!" she says, smiling; "I knew you'd come-to."

"And now where shall we go to?" I asks her.

"O, to Hampton Court," she answers; "Mr. and Mrs. Wilson, and Polly Edwards and her young man, and some more people from hereabout are going, and they wanted another couple to make up the number for the van, and so I took the seats."

"O, that's it, is it?" I says.

"Yes, that's it, my dear," she answers, again laughing; "I thought I might as well take them at once, for I knew it would be all right when I mentioned it to you."

"You knew you intended to have your own way, you mean, I suppose?" says I.

"Well, yes, if you like," she says, keeping on laughing. "You know, Bill, when we were married I didn't say love, honour, and *obey*, but love, honour, and have my own way; so I'm bound to have it, to keep my promise."

"You generally manage to get it, anyway," I says, "promise or no promise."

"And what if I do, Bill?" she asks, looking up in my face, and speaking quite coaxing like; "it ain't such a bad way after all, is it now?"

"That it ain't, my lass," I says; "it would be a good job for working men (and it's true, though perhaps I shouldn't say it), if there was more like you."

"Well, I daresay it would," she says, getting up and beginning to clear away the dinner-things; "but the holiday's settled, isn't it?"

"O, yes, it's settled," I answers; "and as I am going in for it, you needn't be afraid but what I'll go in with a will."

And settled it was; for on the Monday morning off we goes, Bessie looking her best, and dressed up to the nines, in a little top-knot bonnet and a zebra-patterned dress, and her gloves on, and carrying a blue parasol. When we got to "The help me through the World" (shown by the picture of one fellow trying to pull another through a globe), the public as the van was to start from, all the party were there except Polly Edwards and her young man, and in a few minutes they came up; Polly, who is in the dress-making line and knows all about the fashions, sweeping along the street all a swell, with no crinoline, and her dress dragging a yard behind her, and her hair frizzed in front, and a chignon about the size of a young bolster at the back.

"Good-morning, Mr. Banks," she says, shaking hands with me quite polite; "allow me to introduce my young gentleman—Mr. Smith, Mr. Banks."

"How do, Mr. Smith?" I says.

"Pretty tidy, thank you," says he.

"Beautiful day, ain't it?" says I; "what do you say if we have a wet before we start?"

"I don't mind," he says; and so we turned in and had a pint of ale, and then we all got into the van and rattled off, the children in the street giving us a cheer, and the cornet-player that was with us playing "Slap-bang."

Well, we got to Hampton all right, except for a little bit of a squabble between Polly's young man and the musician, who got playing "The ugly Donkey-cart," which, seeing as our turn-out wasn't over and above spicy, wasn't quite the thing; for, as Polly's chap said, it would give people the pull of us if it came to a chaffing match; and so, after a deal of persuasion, we got him to play "The King of Trumps," instead.

The owner of the van had contracted to supply us with a good dinner at half-a-crown a-head, and was to have it all ready at three o'clock, in a nice quiet spot near the Wilderness, which he showed us how to find the way to; and so when we got to the Palace about eleven o'clock, as we all knew where to meet again, and didn't want to look like a lot of yokels, we broke up into parties,—Polly and her chap, and Bessie and me, going together. We went through the different rooms, a-looking at the pictures and painted ceilings, and all that, and very nice they was, though we couldn't quite understand some of 'em, 'specially the ceilings, which were all gods and goddesses, and cupids, and them sort of people as you read about in old poetry-books, and see in the statues at the Crystal Palace, and as I don't believe ever was in reality. However, we couldn't stay to look at 'em very particular, as it took us all our time looking pretty sharp to get through all the rooms by dinner-time.

The dinner was a first-rater—beef and mutton and ham, and any quantity of rolls, and lots of fruit-tarts, in the way of eating, and bottled ale and a small cask of porter to wash 'em down. We were all at the dinner-place to the call of time, and as soon as the last of the lot had come in we set to work, and soon spoiled the looks of the joints and tarts, and made a hole in the porter. Eating and talking at the same time don't generally go well together, and ain't a profitable game, but there's no rule without an exception; and so when I saw, by them beginning to slacken their speed, that all hands had had a good rough filling, I thinks to myself, "It'll be all the more comfortable if we take our time, and have a chat over finishing."

So, by way of making a start, I says, "Well, I never saw such a lot of fine pictures together before, as what's here."

"Well, there's some beautiful ones among them, that's certain," said a young fellow as was out for the day with his intended, "'specially some of the likenesses of ladies; it does a fellow's eyes good to look at 'em."

"Ay," I says, "some of 'em were court beauties in their day, and I daresay gave many a fine swell the heartache."

"Well, if all's true as is said about them, some of them weren't no better than they should have been," says Polly Edwards, quite sharplike.

"Why, as far as that goes, Polly," I made answer, "I fancy there ain't many of us as *are* any better than we should be."

"Well, then, if you *will* be so particular, Mr. Banks," says she, getting quite warm, "they weren't as good as they should have been, not by a long way."

"No, that they weren't," says an old woman with spectacles on, and a face that sour-looking that it's a wonder to me it hadn't turned the porter (she was the mother-in-law of a quiet-looking young chap as was sitting close to me, and as told me afterwards that she led him a regular dog's life)—"No, that they weren't," says she, taking up the conversation quite vicious; "they were a

J. Palmer, del.   Dalziel Bros., sc.

"A HUMAN WAIF CAST UPON THE FINAL SHORE."

pack of trolloping madams as ought to have been
ashamed of themselves; that's what they were."

"Well, that's as may be," I says; "but they're
a handsome-looking lot all the same."

"Handsome, indeed!" she screams out;
"Handsome is as handsome does, say I. What's
the use of having good looks if your behaviour
ain't good too? It ain't good looks as'll save you
at the day of judgment. Beauty is only skin-
deep."

"That's a precious lot more, then," I says,
"than can be said for ugliness, for I'm blest
if that don't often go a deal deeper than the skin:
it gets as far as the temper sometimes."

She was getting the steam up to pitch in again
with something strong; but my Bessie, seeing
that no good was likely to come of it, cut in before
her, by pointing towards the Palace, and saying,
"That's a fine old building; their heads don't
ache that built that."

"No, not if they'd all been Methuselahs,"
says a swell of a fellow as is behind the counter at
the provision-shop at the top of our street. "Why,
it's above a thousand years old. It was built by
the great Admiral Wolsey, and was the grandest
palace in the world at that time. So when the
king—him as cut his wives' heads off, you know
—hears of this, he says to himself, 'I'm blow'd
if this chap doesn't think himself a better man

than me; I must teach him to know who's who.' So he says to him, 'I say, who have you built this 'ere grand palace for?' But Wolsey was a sharp chap, and smelt a rat, and so he says, 'For you, your majesty.' 'O, that's all right, then,' says the king; and he collars the palace, and gives the poor admiral the sack."

Now if the counterman had been swelling the company's heads, I wouldn't have spoiled sport; but seeing that he was quite serious, and thought he had been giving us what the papers call an "intellectual treat," I says, "Well, excuse me, mate, but I think you are rather out in your account of the palace."

"You may *think* what you like," he answers; "but I've read all about it in a guide-book, and you must allow me to *know*."

"Well," I says, "I daresay that all that you know, and all that you *don't* know, would make a big book, only what you don't know would be a long way the largest part of it; and who built Hampton Palace, and when it was built, would be on the don't-know side of the volume; for, just let me tell you, the palace ain't a thousand year old, nor nothing like it; and it wasn't built by *Admiral* Wolsey either. It was a Wolsey that built it, but he was a *Cardinal*."

"Well, I'm blest!" said the counterman; "that's a lot to get contradicting a fellow about;

why, there's only the difference of a letter or two."

"A letter or two makes a good deal of difference sometimes, my boy," I says, "and there's a wide difference between an admiral and a cardinal: the one's a parson, and t'other's a sailor; and you may lay long odds that no sailor could have got round the king, and put the stunners on the court nobs and parliament men of the day the same as this cardinal did."

"Well done, Bill!" says Polly Edwards's young man when I had done. "You talked to him like a book."

"I told him what was right, anyway," I says, "and chance all about the guide-book."

"O, ay, so *you* say," he puts in; "but I should think that a chap like me was more likely to know about a thing of this kind than a fellow as is only a stoker."

"Only a stoker!" cries Bessie, flaring up in an instant. "Only a stoker, indeed! He's a lot better man than you at anything, let me tell you. And as to books, and history, and being a scholard, there's more in his little finger than there is in your whole ugly hulking carcass. What *you* know most about is giving short weight, and palming bad things on to people as ain't good judges."

She rattled into him at such a pace that she

had got thus far before I knew where I was; but now I got my head again, and calls out, "Hold hard, Bessie, my girl; put the break on! May difference of opinion never alter friendship! is the motto you should stick to when you go to argufy; so let him have his opinion, and I'll have mine, and no one will be any the worse."

"Well, you know best, Bill," she says; "but I would let him know what o'clock it was if it was me."

Seeing as how she was still inclined to tell him a piece of her mind, as she calls giving anyone a tongue-dressing, I says to the company, "Well, ladies and gentlemen, as the drink is all out, and everyone seems to have done all they know in the eating line, and somehow we don't seem to hit it off very well talking about the pictures, and the palace, and the like, I vote that we break up again, and have a turn round till it's time to meet for going back."

This was agreed to, and we knocked about the grounds till five o'clock, when we were to start back, as all of us, except Mother Crusty and her unfortunate son-in-law and his wife, had agreed to go to the Alhambra for a wind-up. We started on the return journey all right, the cornet-player giving us "When Johnny comes marching home," and we joining in the chorus, and in due time we found ourselves in the Alhambra.

The performance was very grand; but as there's often accounts of it in the papers, there's no use in me saying anything about it, specially as Bessie tells me as I was asleep when some of the best things were on.

We came out about eleven o'clock, and Polly Edwards's chap says to me, "I'll go yer arves in a four-wheeler, Bill;" and as I felt tired, I says, "All right, mate; only let me make the bargain with cabby, because I know their ways."

"Very well," he says. And so I calls a cabman, and asks him, "How much will you take us four to ——street for?"

"Six shillings," he answered.

"Six shillings be blow'd!" says I. "Three's more like the figure."

"O, I couldn't take you for that," he says, shaking his head.

Well, I wanted to get home; and so, instead of arguing the point, as I would have done at another time, I says to him, "Look here, old chap; I'll toss you whether it's six or three?"

"You're on," says he; "how's it to be?"

"O, sudden death," I says (that's the first toss does it).

"Very well," he says, "you cry;" and he spins up a shilling.

"Woman!" I cries, "if it was for a kingdom."

"Woman it is," he says, showing the coin; "in you jump, three bob's the figure."

Polly lived in the next street to us, and we dropped her and her chap there, and then drove on to our house; and as we went up the street I could see the women coming to the bedroom-windows at the noise of the cab, and I could twig them taking stock of Bessie and me as we were getting out; and thinks I to myself, "O, you good-natured creatures, you'll be having me over the coals nicely to-morrow, and saying that I *must* have been robbing someone, and cabs ain't paid for out of a stoker's wages, and all that; but there's one consolation — when you're on me, you're off some other poor devil, and it's all one to William."

A BIRTHDAY RHYME.

The last Birthday Rhyme.

I.

November brings my darling's day of birth.
   She sleeps in earth;
Her eyes shall never more behold
Soft rains autumnal brimming up
   The bindweed cup,
Or green lime-leafage turning gold.

II.

Upon the damp and leaf-strewn lawn I see
   Her medlar-tree;
Her scarlet oak has ceased to burn;
Her dahlias droop in humid air.
   I know not where
Are those brown eyes for which I yearn.

III.

She cannot take a birthday gift from me,
  Or read with glee
Love's little sheet of foolish rhyme.
Ah, well I know your meaning now,
  Sad winds that blow
Through Autumn's melancholy time.

Steamboating in America.

By Howard Paul.

THE "mighty Thames, the "rushing Dart," and the "placid Avon," are all pretty pet little streams, abounding in the most genial and picturesque landscape scenery that can be imagined; but in the matter of rivers, as is known to every traveller, America possesses some of the largest and most magnificent on the globe. The Amazon, of Brazil; the Ohio, Mississippi, Hudson, and Delaware, of the United States; and the St. Lawrence, on the Canadian borders, are stately specimens of fresh-water grandeur. To set aside the value of these streams in a commercial point of view, and the preëminence they give the country in natural advantages, we cannot be insensible to the varied and numerous pleasures they afford the communities that reside on their banks; and foremost among these may be ranked the steamboat excursions, when the moon is gilding the waters, and the delicate pencil of eventide is touching-up Nature with its " chromo-nocturnal tints of subdued sableness," as poor N. P. Willis used to write.

An American steamboat differs vastly in capability and mode of construction from the French and English contrivances. We can conceive nothing more uncomfortable than a trip to Kew on an ill-looking, dingy Thames boat, crowded to suffocation, with a blazing sun pouring upon your exposed head; or a spasmodic run down the Soane, with nothing to relieve the eye but a group of villas here and there in the neighbourhood of Lyons; or a galvanic voyage on the Rhine, with the black grit from the smoke-pipe perpetually flying in your eyes.

The American steamboats vary in many respects. On the eastern waters they are luxuries; while those of the gigantic Mississippi and western streams are ponderous, unwieldy, and inelegant. A Hudson-river or Delaware boat, without being ungracefully large, possesses just sufficient roominess for all festive purposes; although, in justice to the western craft, we would remark, they are built more with a view to the reception of merchandise than the accommodation of passengers. A vessel may be too large as well as too small; and to our taste the eastern river-boats are just the size to insure beauty and comfort. An American steamboat floats upon the waters as gracefully as a swan. There is an absence of all that dreadful puffing, grunting, and hissing in the mechanical region so calculated to mar the enjoyment of the voyager. She drops down the stream with an easy dignity, and indulges in no unseemly sounds or convulsive jerks. The large pleasure-boats have two, and in some cases three, distinct decks, each appointed with becoming suitableness. The upper or promenade deck (usually about 210 feet in length) is skirted with canechairs and benches, leaving the centre and sides for the purpose which its name suggests. The forward portion of the second deck is apportioned to light articles of merchandise, and is the only place on the boat where smoking is permitted.

Aft on this deck is the ladies' grand cabin, communicating with special cabins, private apartments, and retiring-rooms. Gentlemen are never

allowed to cross these exclusive thresholds, except
in the principal cabin; which privilege is only
granted when they are so fortunate as to have the
companionship of the fair sex. These apartments
are furnished in the most costly and appropriate
manner. Few drawing-rooms in the large cities
exhibit more taste than the ladies' cabins. They
are not over-crowded; but the mirrors, fauteuils,
lounges, sofas, curtains, ottomans, and pianos are
placed at becoming intervals, with a harmony of
arrangement quite artistic. The severest connois-
seur of decorative art could take no exception to the
want of keeping. The gentlemen's cabin is substantially furnished, with this unimportant differ-
rence, that the carpet is not so choice in pattern and
quality as that the ladies are permitted to press;
and this, we fancy, arises from the predisposition
of American gentlemen to indulge in reckless
expectoration, without "aim or the fear of consequence," as somebody has expressed it. We find
here no beautiful Sèvres vases filled with blooming
flowers, occupying the graceful angles of the apartment; but in lieu of these, sturdy round tables
covered with papers. Ladies and flowers, men
and newspapers, are consistent associations. The
chairs may not be as velvety and elegant as those
" 'tother sex" are permitted to occupy; but when
it is remembered that the gentlemen feel no compunction at elevating their toes on a line with

their noses—particularly in a political dispute as to who ought to be President of the United States —the difference is reasonable enough.

The basement cabins are divided off in systematic style for the purpose of dining, lounging, and drinking. Each boat is thoughtfully provided with a bar and barber's-shop, where the fatigued traveller can have his whiskers curled in one, and the cobwebs removed from his throat in the other, with a spirit of accommodativeness quite delightful under the circumstances. These are conveniences that reflect credit upon the tact and management of the conductors, whoever they may be, and which render "making one's way" on an American steamboat quite a matter of pleasure as well as progress.

The excellence of a steamboat-dinner is a proverb; their cooks, *cuisine*, and waiters are all *marqué au bon coin*. The cooks are fatter, the waiters more deferential "ten times over," the tablecloth whiter, and the comestibles better than can be found anywhere else; and these are all great points. One's gastronomic longings are never put to the blush by a tortured *relevé* in the shape of a bilious-looking jambon, and the chickens have not that hard, dry, done-a-long-time-ishness appearance that frightens appetite, as fantastic scarecrows will put to flight the boldest of birds. Completeness reigns throughout. The napkins are folded until they resemble cambric cartoons; the salt-cellars, and their excellent friends the pepper-boxes, are never out of your reach; and if a porringer that you desire meet not your finger-tips, the merest effort in the world will secure it. After fasting, should invalids desire a change and a "good dinner," the *salle à manger* of the steamboat is their resort; and a serviceable one it will be found.

It is the moonlight excursions that exhibit the American steamboat in all its glory. The neatly-painted decks have been washed, the promenades arranged, the cabins set to rights, and, in short, every article aboard seems determined to put on its best looks for the occasion. The excursion is, say, twenty miles, to a pleasant country town; the month August; and the moon is supposed to smile brightly and delightfully on every object terrestrial. A brass and string band of considerable force is engaged; coloured lights are suspended here and there with a view both to light and effect; the waiters (mostly negroes) have made themselves very smart; and the extra bar-keepers of the "lower cabin" are up to their whiskers in bunches of mint, lemons, pine-apples, peaches, and "the wherewithal" to construct those wonderful fancy tipples only found on the other side of the Atlantic.

The boat in question is called the Star of the

Waters, the Americans revelling in pretty titles for their conveyances, and she has advertised to leave the pier at half-past eight precisely, in order to return, if possible, by midnight,—a judicious arrangement to please the anxious mammas of various young ladies who may wish to " trip it on the light fantastic toe" by the light of the moon.

The price of the trip is one dollar for a gentleman and two ladies; another thoughtful arrangement, which secures a large admixture of the fair sex, and gives elegance and sprightliness to the entertainment on board.

It is an animated scene. How the ladies smile and laugh as they flit over the promenades! Here is a coquette, with sparkling eye, getting up a flirtation with a handsome friend of her beau's, just to tease the poor fellow. There is a group of girls in undulating muslin, with pink sashes and fair ringlets, all in the gayest of humours. The captain of the boat is talking with a charming young lady, lavishly attired, who has just arrived, and who, we feel confident, will establish herself as the belle of the night before the "witching hour" arrives. What an array of demi-toilettes, skirts of every hue, and bodices fashioned with exquisite skill; head-dresses, from a single white flower in the hair to the sparkling tiara of jewels!

The tickets are all in (to use a professional

phrase of the boat), and with majestic quietude the Star hauls off into the stream, and sets her bow towards her rustic destination. Viewing her from the pier, how magnificent the spectacle! The lights beam in roseate beauty, myriad forms in the wildest glee are stirring about the decks, the sounds of the music steal over the waters, the waves ripple joyously by, the queen of the night rides serenely in the heavens, and all tells of festivity and happiness.

We watch the boat until it is out of sight. The lights fade gradually away; the strains of the music die gently upon the air; no more we hear the soft plash of the waves. The excursionists have gone, and are now mingling in the mazes of the quadrille, and "making love" in the lustre of the moonbeams. Happy creatures!

Alfred Slader, del. Dalziel Bros., sc.

FALLING LEAVES.

THE DEVIL-TREE.

BY JAMES GREENWOOD.

A DEVIL-TREE, as might be expected, is of different aspect from any other tree that grows.

It is usually a tree of gigantic growth, and sound and green as any of its forest brethren. It is its fruit that makes it so singular a spectacle. As everybody is aware, the vegetable productions of the dominion of the King of Mascat are marvellous to behold. Little bushes are bowed to the ground with scarlet orange-shaped fruit as large as cocoa-nuts; and trees bigger than English beeches present the appearance of a giant bouquet, being literally covered with tiny waxen white flowers, delicate as the jonquil and fragrant as the rose. Grape-like bunches of delicious-looking fruit festoon the highway hedges in far greater abundance than blackberries on English bushes, and hang and rot; for so deadly poisonous are they, that a bullet through the head would not be more fatal than one of these grapes in the mouth.

But the most curious tree of all is the one that from its bole to its topmost branch is festooned with rags and scraps and flinders of every possible description. Little parcels of dried grass, screws of matting pinned through with a thorn, scraps of cask-hooping, broken bottles, splinters of wood, old pots and pans, wisps of straw, fag-ends of rope, and a hundred other things beside.

This is "the devil-tree." Every district of Zanzibar possesses one; indeed, its existence is as essential to the lives of the inhabitants—that is, the native inhabitants—as their daily bread. There is no such thing as doing without the devil-tree; and yet the jet-black, woolly-headed believers in it pass by it with fear and trembling, and can scarcely look on it without a shudder. And no wonder; it is a hive of imps. Of the thousand devils that afflict the good people of Zanzibar, there is not one but has its representative housed in this tree. Imps of plague live there, imps of famine, small-pox imps, yellow-fever imps, and imps that afflict men with raving madness. These are there, and many more, all alive, and ready to hop down and begin their old tricks anew,

if ever they should grow dissatisfied with their lot.
That innocent-looking stone bottle, handleless,
spoutless, and with a great rent in its side, is the
house of an imp, whose diabolical mission it is to
break men's limbs. That bit of crooked iron hoop,
gibbeted to yon big bough, looks perfectly harm-
less, but invisibly astride it, or on it, or somewhere about it, is an imp of the blackest dye,
no less, indeed, than a murder imp. His history
is soon stated. He took possession of a man and
caused him to break his wife's head with a club,
and to strangle his two little children and throw
them into the river. True, they hanged the man
for it, but they could not kill the wicked imp that
still lurked within his inanimate body; so his
friends coaxed the dead man of the hangman, and
conjured the dreadful little demon into that bit of
iron hoop, and hung him up in the devil-tree. The
bit of iron hoop was not so withered-looking at
the time the man was hanged as it is now. It
was quite a new bit of hoop, and the imp must
have procured it for the prisoner out of the
king's store. At all events, they had caught the
wretch with it on the morning of his execution,
and he had ground it as sharp as a razor against
a stone, for the purpose of taking his own life, it
was thought, but his courage failed him. When
his friends fetched the body home, they were a
little perplexed as to which the imp would choose

as his future abode—the club with which he had killed his wife, or the bit of iron hoop. They laid both implements on the dead man's breast, and the mystery-man and the musicians, with their reed whistles and their copper bangers and their tom-toms, sat round him, and played all the prettiest tunes they knew. It was plain, from the length of time the imp kept the musicians at work, that he was undecided as to whether the club or the bit of iron hoop should be his future abode; but presently the mystery-doctor observed the bit of iron hoop quiver, and of course that settled the question.

So every rag, tag, and flinder attached to the devil-tree has its story. Some are so very old, that the particular atrocity for which the imp dwelling therein was captured and condemned to the evil tree is forgotten; but the tree is of gigantic size, and the imps' houses may be counted by hundreds. A middle-aged man, beginning that tree's history, could scarcely hope to finish it before the death-imp caught him napping, and stopped his breath. It will be better, therefore, to be moderate, and select but one of the thousand imps' houses, only one. Which shall it be? Here, hanging by a stout iron chain, which is bound firmly round it, is what appears to be a dirty-white rag, rotten through long exposure. Let us question the priest of the tree concerning it.

"Is it in the rag or in the chain that this particular imp has its lodging?"

"In the rag," replies the mystery-man, in a frightened whisper.

"In the rag! but why is it necessary to secure so flimsy a thing with a chain strong enough to hold a ship at her moorings? A piece of bark-cord would do quite as well."

"Ah, there you are mistaken," says the mystery-man solemnly; "so powerful a devil lives in that cloth that any fastening less strong than an iron chain would be insufficient to hold him. He would break away and be among us again in a minute."

"Anyhow, he cannot be a very big imp; there is nowhere for him to lodge but in the knot that attaches the rag to the chain."

"Ah, but he is not all in one," replies the priest, in a whisper so low that to catch what he says it is necessary to incline your ear towards his lips, "he is not all in one; he is spread about in spots—yellow spots."

"But where are the yellow spots? I can't see any."

"Hush! he is so cunning, that is the reason; when he was first hung up you could see his spots a long way off. This was so until last winter, and the season of rain and wind. When we then came to look, what we could see of the cloth was without spots, and we said, 'The wet and the cold have starved him out; he does not like wet and cold; he likes to lie snug and warm; he has left us. We may take down his ugly house and burn it!' I thought so too; so I got a fetish ladder to climb up and unhook the chain; but as I was about to do it, the thought came into my head that I had better make sure; so I took the folds of the rag-shreds in my fingers and pulled them apart and peeped in. It was lucky that I did so. He was there all the time, hiding within the knot. There were his yellow spots to be seen quite plain. What an escape! No doubt he is tired of hanging up there, and would be glad to be amongst us again at his horrible work."

Surely we cannot do better than elect for recital the story of the imp with the yellow spots.

"How old he is no man knows," says the mystery-man. "Nobody in Zanzibar recollects seeing him before, but some of the gray-bearded say that they have heard their fathers speak of this spotted devil, how he came among them devouring them by hundreds. If this was so, he must be very old—a hundred years old, at least; and truly he did go about his work like one used to it.

"He came amongst us just four years ago. It was in the middle of the hot season, and the rice was ready for gathering, and the harvesters were out. All the males of the village were abroad; so that when the spotted imp came and looked about him, and peeped into the huts, some he found empty, and at best nobody but women and children. At last he came to a hut in which sat, grinding corn, a young woman whose husband was out in the fields, and there he tarried.

"She was singing when the spotted imp entered, but in a little while she became silent and sick-looking; and though the sun was blazing at its highest, she began to shiver as though it were winter-time. For a little while she tried to bear up, never dreaming of the frightful thing that had possession of her. At last she was obliged to lay down the grinding-stone, and sit down with her head resting on her knees.

"By and by it grew towards middle day, when she should have carried the water-bottle to her husband. He waited and waited, and finding she did not come, he slipped out of the field, and hurried home to see what was the matter.

"She was still sitting with her head on her knees when he entered, and thinking she had fallen asleep, in a passion he lifted his foot to kick her; but just in time she raised her face towards him, and his anger was at once turned to terror and amazement. Her face was so altered: her eyes were sparkling like fire, her lips were pinched away from her teeth, and her cheeks and her forehead and her breast were covered with little round spots the colour of gold.

"To all his questions she could answer nothing; so he called to one of his neighbours, and told him to fetch me; and when I came, the hut was full of women, busying themselves about the afflicted one, and trying to rouse her. This was a fine chance for the spotted imp, who made the most of it, as you shall presently hear.

"It was plain that the unlucky creature was possessed, and, turning out the women, I sent for the musicians, and we laid her down, and began the task of driving the imp out of her. It was some time before I could make up my mind which bait was best to catch it. Ascertaining how the woman was engaged, I at once ordered that some half-ground meal should be put in a bag and laid on her breast, thinking it likely that, being hungry, the imp had smelt the meal as he passed the door, and entered to take some, but that, being alarmed, he had jumped down the woman's throat to save himself.

"But though we drummed and beat the gong our hardest, and played on our whistles the most seductive tunes, the obstinate imp would not leave the woman, at least so we thought; but when we had played for two hours and more, there was a loud knocking at the door, and in came a young man to tell us that it was of no use us trying to catch the spotted imp in that place, for at that very moment his old mother was possessed of him, and lying at death's door.

"Hurrying to the hut where the young man's mother lived, we found it just as he had stated. There lay the woman with the same blazing eyes, the same pinched lips, and the same spots of the colour of gold on her cheeks and her forehead and her breast. Instantly I recognised her as one of the women whom I had found in the hut along with the harvester's wife when I first entered it, and consequently was able to account at once for a circumstance otherwise mysterious. The old woman, while bending over the young one, had attracted the malicious imp, and he had fastened on to her.

"Now, thought we, we cannot fail to catch him; so we took our places, and at once began to drum and whistle; but scarcely had we commenced, when there came a knocking at this door as at the other. Another old woman was possessed of the yellow imp; and scarcely had this messenger told his tale, when still another made his appearance, breathless and in affright; and then one more, and still another, treading close on his heels, all in one voice clamouring the dreadful story, that the devil with the yellow spots had taken up his abode in their house.

"It was plain there was something more than

mystery in this: there was witchcraft. I told the people, as I appealed to them, to say if they had ever known me to fail in exorcising an evil spirit. I challenged them to show me an imp of the common sort, who could withstand my powers. This, however, was no common imp; it was an imp capable of being in twenty places at one time, and under such circumstances it was impossible to cope with him. They asked my advice, and I gave it them. It would be better, I told them, to hunt for the witch who was assisting the imp, and so to crush the mischief at its fountain-head.

"Meanwhile the yellow-spotted devil had all its own way. With the swiftness of the wind he hurried from hut to hut, firing the eyes of young and old, pinching their lips, and branding their breasts and foreheads with the blurry spot of gold colour. To be so branded was to be impressed with the seal of death. Not one escaped. In nine days four hundred, little and big, were carried out, and thrown into the pit. Had the yellow imp retained his liberty for nine days more, there would scarcely have been a live man left. Day by day the mischief increased, so that if sixty died to-day, a hundred would die to-morrow, and a hundred and fifty the day after. But, fortunately, a sudden stop was put to the horrible pranks the imp was playing. The witch, who was assisting the imp to appear in a hundred and fifty places at one time, was discovered.

"It was the witch's own son who found him out. We never thought that he possessed witch-power, but regarded him as a poor old man who got his living by the river, helping to load the merchantmen's boats. Not one of us but would have been bound for the old man's harmlessness; but this, of course, only showed the deep cunning of his witch-nature, and of the intensity of the malice which actuated him.

"It was in the night he was found out. Suddenly there was a loud noise in the street, mingled with prayers and entreaties for mercy. Less noise would have served to rouse the town, and out rushed the people to see what the matter was. There they saw the old boat-porter lying on the ground, and his son, who was a great strong fellow, dragging him along by one of his arms. It was a moonlight night; and they likewise could see that the old porter, who was very small and shrunken, was imp-struck. They saw that his eyes gleamed, and that his lips were pinched back from his teeth, and that his forehead and his cheeks and breast were blurred with the terrible colour. When they saw that he was so afflicted, some of the people raised an outcry at what they thought was great cruelty on the part of the son, and bade him desist from serving his father in a manner so scandalous,

and even threatened him; but by the utterance of
a few simple words he instantly made them alter
their tone. 'He is the witch,' said he; 'he is
the wicked wretch who is leagued with the spotted
imp to kill us all. He carries about with him the
house in which the imp with the yellow spots
lives.' When the people heard this, they set up
a loud yell of execration, and would instantly have
fallen on the monster, and torn him limb from
limb, had they not been afraid of approaching him
too closely. As it was, the son began to drag the
old man through the dust towards my hut, the
mob following behind and pelting him with stones.

"Now, I had known the son to be a very
ignorant fellow, and, hearing how matters stood,
resolved to act cautiously, and not convict his
father without substantial evidence. It was not
wanting. I came out of my hut, and before the
people, who gathered in a great ring, I bade the
old man cease his clamour, while his son stated
the charge against him.

"'This night,' said he, 'as I lay asleep with
my father in his hut, he awoke me, and said, 'My
son, I am ill; the yellow-spotted one has fastened
on me, and I shall die. I am poor, and have
no wealth to leave thee—nothing but this. Long
have I hoarded it secretly; now it shall be thine.'
What it was my father offered me he bade me
search for under his girdle, whence I took it; but

as soon as I saw it, I thrust it back again, and there it is now.'

"As the old man lay panting on the ground, I thrust my hand where the son pointed, and there I found it—the cloth with the yellow spots—the same that hangs up in the tree till this day, bound by an iron chain. There was no mistaking it: there were the blurry spots, in every one of which, doubtless, lived one of the vindictive imps. Nevertheless, and although the mob stood round with great stones in their hands, yelling and howling for his destruction, I thought it but just to ask the old witch what he had to say.

"'There is no witch in it,' says he; 'a year and more ago, a sailor-man gave it to me, and I have never worn it because it was too fine. I offered it to my son because I had nothing else to leave him, and that he might remember me.'

"Was it a wonder, when the people heard him utter this ridiculous excuse, that their wrath waxed hotter than ever; that in their mad fury they forgot even their respect for me? They bade me stand aside, unless I too would be stoned; and hurled their missiles at the witch till his body was beaten into the ground. They burnt down his hut, and dragged his body from under the stones which were heaped on it, and threw it on the red-hot embers of his hut, and it was consumed. They then took the spotted devil-house and hung it on the tree, and purified their huts, and bathed in the sea, as is their custom after having been delivered from a great calamity.

"From that time there were fewer deaths from yellow spot, and in a little while the plague ceased entirely."

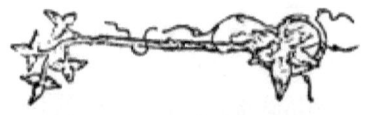

WATER BABIES.

The Time will come.

BY FRANK YOUNGE.

I.

"The time will come!" these simple words
    A world of varied meaning tell,—
Now merry as the song of birds,
    Now mournful as a passing bell.
The child—who longing to be free
    To roam the sunny woods and fields,
Where rippling streams flow on in glee,
    And Nature store of fragrance yields—
When all his heart makes holiday,
    And bees o'er blooming flow'rets hum,
Doth, hopeful of his freedom, say,
    "The time will come—the time will come!"

II.

"The time will come!" aspiring cries,
    With throbbing heart and soul aflame,
The ardent youth who vows to rise,
    Till he has won an envied name,
When his renown aloft shall shine
    Like some proud star above the sea,
To all the world a brilliant sign
    That he hath gain'd the victory:
For ever to his eager soul,
    Like sound of "spirit-stirring drum,"
These accents, full of promise, roll—
    "The time will come—the time will come!"

III.

"The time will come!" the maiden fair
    Has murmur'd, in her bloom of youth,
In hope the future time to share
    With one who vow'd her life-long truth.
Alas, alas, that such things are!
    Her idol proves but worthless clay,
Who, deeming gold more precious far,
    Her priceless love has cast away.
But shall he scatheless do this deed?
    No, conscience never will be dumb:
For him repentance shall succeed;
    "The time will come—the time will come!"

IV.

"The time will come," the patriot cries,
    "When men shall do me justice here:
Which though my native land denies,
    Not less is she my country dear.
When force and fraud would trample low
    Her liberties amid the dust,
My life-blood in her cause shall flow,
    And prove me worthy of her trust.
Those hearts shall do me justice then
    That Falsehood now has stricken numb,
Yet shall they rise to truth again:
    The time will come—the time will come!"

V.

"The time will come!"—a captive's hope,
    Who, gazing through his prison-bars,
Surveys the distant azure cope
    Where shine the soft and pitying stars.
He thinks of home, and those who pine
    To hold him to their hearts once more:
Where wife and children's pray'rs combine
    To hail his cruel bondage o'er.
Though, haply, Death alone may be
    His liberator, yet the sum
Of all his hopes thus whispers he—
    "The time will come—the time will come!"

VI.

"The time will come!" the weary heart,
    Worn by its conflict with the world,
Sighs, as though longing to depart
    For realms where Sorrow's wings are furl'd,
Where Falsehood cannot enter in,
    Where love and friendship ne'er grow cold,
But perfect truth and beauty win
    Each heart within their tender fold.
To meet again the loved and lost,
    To hear those tones Death bade be dumb,
We pray—though here so tempest-tost—
    "The time will come—the time will come!"

F. Barnard, del.　　　Dalziel Bros., sc.

CATCHING DABS.

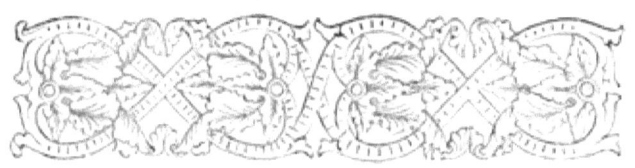

Three Hundred and Four.

BY GEORGE AUGUSTUS SALA.

> "Nessun maggior piacere
> Che ricordarsi, nel tempo felice,
> Della miseria." *Anonymous.*

BUT was it misery? Well, it was poverty; and are not poverty and misery one and the same thing?

Understand me: I do not call him poor who has enough of anything:—be it truffles and Chambertin, or tripe and onions, or bread and cheese. "We can be good and happy without socks," poor Robert Brough made his erratic philosopher Billy Barlow say; but Barlow had never felt the want of socks. Had he worn them, they might have impeded the freedom of his march, the independence of his port. Barlow was a nomad, a quagga kind of man; restless, incult, but happy. Because Pocahontas had never known the luxury of a chemise she was not less Princess of Virginia.

To be very poor is to be very miserable; and to be very miserable is, I hold, a very beneficial mental and bodily state for any man to be in. To have wanted bread and raiment and a bed now and then in the course of your career, should tend—if you have a man's heart in you, and not a beast's—to make you, if you attain prosperity, tolerant and charitable, and passably humble and grateful. For all your fine horses and carriages, and money in the funds, you may be a beggar again some day. There is your incentive to humility. Spurn not that mendicant; set him not down sternly as an impostor: you were yourself quite innocent of imposture when you were needy and sought relief. There is your incentive to charity. Don't be angry with the poor devil who worries you with the begging-letter. You *were* expecting a remittance when you wrote to Dives requesting the favour of that small loan. You *did* intend to repay him, with grateful thanks. You *had* pawned your coat. You had *not* tasted food for two days when you waited, sick at heart, at the foot of his staircase for an answer, or were repulsed by his lacqueys from his outward rooms. Now, how is a man to understand poverty, and to appreciate want, and to pity necessity, if he have not been himself one of the *bisognosi*—if he have not himself gone through the slow-grinding mill of utter penury? There never were two more charitable men than Oliver Goldsmith and Samuel Johnson, and there had seldom been, in their earlier days, two needier ones. 'Twas the remembrance of the time when he lived among the beggars of Axe-lane—when he pawned the suit of clothes the publisher had obtained for him on credit—when he left his Bishop-visitor Warburton in Green Arbour-court to lend the Irishwoman below a slop-basin full of coals—that opened Oliver's hand when he came to wear silk stockings and a coat of Tyrian bloom, that moved him to enrol that band of small pensioners who made a more solemn show when he lay dead in the Temple than all the Gentlemen Pensioners could make at the obsequies of a king. 'Twas mindfulness of hunger and nakedness and cold—of nights passed with Savage, wandering up and down the cruel streets, or crouching upon tradesmen's bulks — of the spunging-house and the twopenny ordinary—of the time when he devoured his victuals behind a screen, because, in his ragged horseman's coat, he was not deemed fit to sit at meat with Mr. Cave's grand company —that stirred the grand heart of Johnson to infinite tenderness and pity—that bade him open his house and purse to the fractious blind woman and the silly, troublesome apothecary—that led him to take up the fainting, perishing drab on his back, and bear her to where there was shelter. Did you ever see Murillo's picture of San Juan de Dios? Well, an engraving may serve your turn. The painting is at Seville, in the church of La Caridad — Don Juan's church. The saint has found a beggar, perishing in the gutter, as Johnson found the wanton. Forthwith he hoists him on his shoulders. But the holy man is old and weak, and he staggers, and is falling beneath the load, when an angel comes out of the darkness of the night—an angel with shining face and wings, and cheers him up, and props his arm, and guides his footsteps with his charge, to the 'spital. When I first looked on this picture, I thought at once of Dr. Johnson and the drab.

Do you think, if those wise gentlemen of the House of Commons—many of them *really* wise, generous, charitable according to their lights—had known anything of absolute, grinding, crust-wanting poverty, they would have passed that stupid clause in the Street-Traffic Act which bade fair to deprive thirty thousand costermongers of their means of existence? I am ready to believe that Parliament is far more willing to help a man to earn his bread than to try to starve him; but the M.P.'s sinned, not of malice, but of ignorance. There is a great talk of working-men as representatives of their class in Parliament. Ay, but

I hold that the *bisognosi* should be likewise represented—that the Blind Beggar of Bethnal Green should have his say as well as the guardians and the rate-payers.

Twenty years ago, more or less—more, I think; it was just after the great Railway Mania of '45— I first became acquainted with Three Hundred and Four. It was a shop then, and it is a shop now; but the merchandise sold there is of a far different kind from that which was dispensed in my day. Three Hundred and Four is in the W.C. district, is at the corner of a narrow street, and is not a hundred miles from the church of St. Clement Danes, or of St. Mary-le-Strand, whichever you may choose to fix upon. I will not more minutely particularise. I pass that street-corner almost every day of my life, and salute Three Hundred and Four as an old mournful friend. The shop will always be associated in my mind with my first entrance into the career of letters, and with the extremest poverty. I had elected to " earn my own living," and have my own home, and " be my own master ;" and I shudder sometimes to think of the anguish I have endured.

It *was* anguish, and of the bitterest. It is vastly fine for Béranger to sing, " *Dans un grenier qu'on est bien à vingt ans.*" But how is it when, at twenty years, the garret is lacking, or you are locked out by the landlady for not paying the rent? Béranger talks of his Lisette, of his credit at Madame Grégoin's cabaret, of his pledging his watch to defray the cost of a carouse. How is it when you have no Lisette, no wine-shop-keeper to trust you, no watch to pledge? Béranger had a trade ; he was a compositor, and a working-man need never starve. But in the days I speak of, I could do nothing that would secure me a regular livelihood. I could not draw, or engrave, or paint, or write well enough—although I dabbled in all those crafts—to be received as a skilled journeyman in any workshop. I was that which is very coarsely but very expressively termed a "duffer," that is to say, an incapable, and my services were not worth a pound a-week to any employer.

I know that it has often turned me sick when I have gone into a tavern for half a pint of porter to see a swaggering customer throw down a sovereign, and rattle the great shining half-crowns as he put them up in his fob. I had early fallen a slave to Tobacco—the great consoler, the great afflicter, the merciless usurer, who exacts higher interest each time he renews the bill, and at last claims his capital, and sells you up, and leaves you bankrupt in nerve and brain. I know that when I have not had the means of purchasing a solitary "screw" of bird's-eye, and have searched all my short pipes in the fruitless hope of finding in some forgotten bowl a remnant of "mundungus," I have experienced a miserable pleasure in walking in the street behind a gentleman who was smoking a good cigar, and that the aroma drove me into a kind of sensuous incoherence that was half satisfaction and half despair. I know that I have walked down to Club-land—have wandered up and down Pall Mall and Waterloo-place and St. James's-street, and have gazed, in summer time, through the open windows of the great gas-lit palaces, and have wondered whether the stout gray-headed gentlemen I saw throned before the clean white damask, plying their knives and forks, or sipping their wine, or lounging behind newspapers, belonged to a superior race of mortals—whether they walked and talked like other folks. I have been deferential to the club-porter, and have moved away uneasily when I thought the eyes of one of the club flunkeys were upon me. There is a portrait of a general officer visible from the street in one of the saloons of the Senior United Service, and there are some red-backed chairs you can see through the windows of the Travellers', which affect me strangely to this day.

The times I lived in were prior to the epoch of what is termed, I scarcely know why, Bohemianism. At least, I belonged to no Bohemian clique; and I remember that I once addressed a very distinguished man of letters, who I am given to understand was one of the magnates of Bohemia, as "Sir." I thought him a very grand fellow indeed, who passed a merry life over broiled bones and soda-and-brandy. My city of Prague was in my own garret, and I often felt inclined to cast myself from the window thereof, "after the Bohemian fashion."*

There is much, of course, in the mere fact of youth that aids the poor young man in enduring hardship. He can "rough it" well enough at twenty. His heart may give him a twitch now and then—although I doubt whether any male ever falls really in love before thirty; girls begin at ten—but he is rarely, unless he be a victim to hereditary disease, aware that he has a liver and kidneys or lungs. The "extra glass" may give him a splitting headache the next morning; but later in life every "extra glass" brings with it more than headache—a bushel of coffin-nails. When you are young, you may exceed for a week at the cost of a day's uneasiness; when you are old, you cannot exceed for a day under the penalty of a week's torture. Only an elderly bibber

---

* In the Middle Ages, when the citizens of Prague quarrelled with their burgomasters, they were accustomed to heave them out of the Townhall windows; another deputation of citizens stood beneath and considerately received the falling magistrates on the points of pikes, to prevent their hurting themselves by collision with the pavement. This was called doing justice "after the Bohemian fashion."

could have written those terrible lines we find in *Elia:* "To be an object of compassion to friends, of derision to foes; to be suspected by strangers, stared at by fools; to be esteemed dull when you cannot be witty; to be applauded for witty when you know that you have been dull; to be called upon for the extemporaneous exercise of that faculty which no premeditation can give; to be spurred to efforts which end in contempt; to be set on to provoke mirth which procures the procurer hatred; to give pleasure, and to be paid with squinting malice; to swallow draughts of life-destroying wine, which are to be distilled into airy breath to tickle vain auditors; to mortgage miserable morrows for nights of madness; to waste whole seas of time on those who pay it back in little inconsiderable drops of grudging applause—are the wages of buffoonery and death." Young Bibo is rarely called upon for the "extemporaneous exercise of that faculty which no premeditation can give." He does not swallow draughts of life-destroying wine; he can rarely afford it; and the pots of beer he drinks do not do him much harm, and his excess in potations is generally combined with hard exercise and horseplay, and what is termed "larking." A young sot, a "boozer" at twenty, is a monster.

There are moments, Mr. Thackeray tells us in *Esmond,* when the conversation of a pretty lass

and a flask of champagne in a tavern form the
summum bonum of felicity to the mind of a very
young man. The enjoyment of champagne and
the conversation of pretty lasses imply the possession of money. The very poor young man is
fain to substitute for them a pipe of tobacco, a
pint of beer, and the conversation of young men
as poor as he. This last is more difficult to obtain
in England than in France. The starving young
fellows in Henri Mürger's *Vie de Bohême* make
each other's acquaintance at cafés and eating-
houses easily; no formal introduction is needed;
but in this country the streak of caste is on every
brow, from that of the Blood-Royal Prince to that
of the costermonger. The country sparrow is not
received, without proper credentials, by the town
sparrow. The pauper in "the House" thinks
himself above the pauper in the Casual Ward.
Drunken people at tavern-bars sometimes fore-
gather; but the poor young man rarely forms ac-
quaintances in the taproom, which he is sometimes
forced to frequent, because he yearns to hear the
voice of his fellow-men, and to sit in a warm,
bright room, and because he is not a member of
the Carthaginian Club, Pall Mall. Old Soakesby,
who is a member of that palatial establishment,
has his taproom in the smoking-room of the club,
where he drinks four glasses of hot grog after
dinner. He, too, desires a warm, bright room.

The conversation of his fellow-men Soakesby does not care much for.

On the whole, I am inclined to think that the poor young man can endure occasional alcoholic excess better than he can endure hunger. When you are young, you care very little about being in rags. You make jokes about the dilapidated state of your hat and boots. Society does not yet insist upon your putting on a clean shirt every day. But it is in the belly—to be paradoxical—that the shoe pinches. Young men have such deuced good appetites. I hear an infinity of fine talk about "gross and carnal appetites," and the like; but if you were to take a rigid moralist, or a serene philosopher, or Mr. Matthew Arnold, with his "sweetness," and his "light," and his "culture," and shut him up in a room for three days without any victuals, you would hear him roar like a bull-calf for food. The poor young man's healthy stomach roars within him for meat. To be hungry when you are young, without the means of satisfying your craving, is absolute physical agony; and I have always maintained that the schoolmaster or schoolmistress who would strive to punish a growing child by stinting it in its food is guilty of diabolical cruelty.

Three Hundred and Four! Three Hundred and Four! you are accountable for all these thoughts; for within your precincts did I first learn to think.

We sold Literature at Three Hundred and Four. We published an *Illustrated Journal of Facts, Fun, Fiction, and On Dits;* we sold it at the not immoderate price of one halfpenny. The "Trade" had a discount of five-and-twenty per cent on their purchases, and "thirteen as twelve" in the quire, I think. We were very deferential to the Trade. My heart used to go pit-a-pat when on Monday morning the men and boys with their bags came into the shop, and peremptorily delivered their commissions from Fleet-street and Paternoster-row. It made a great difference, I can assure you, if they wanted four instead of two "quires," for the Trade always paid on the nail, and jingled their shillings and halfpence over the counter in a most inspiriting manner. I wonder whether Mr. George Vickers is aware that he has frequently been the means of supplying the present writer with a mutton-chop. I used to edit the *Illustrated Weekly Journal of Fun, Fact, Fiction, and On Dits.* I drew political caricatures for it. I wrote in it a most appalling romance, several small jokes, much bad poetry, and a series of essays of a highly philosophical tendency. Eventually I became one of Three Proprietors of the Journal. Our united capital, I believe, amounted to seven pounds ten shillings. My earnings as editor and contributor varied between eighteen shillings and twenty-two shillings a week.

But, long prior to my promotion to the editorial throne—which was a three-legged stool behind the counter—I had hung about the office in search of a "job," precisely as an "odd man" might hang about a city warehouse or a dock-gate. Sometimes I got eighteenpence for a joke. Sometime the price of three stanzas of comic poetry rose to three shillings and sixpence. Very frequently the then Proprietor was in difficulties, secreted himself in adjoining ambushes and paid nobody. On those days I starved: not figuratively, but literally. I remember that on the 10th of April 1848 I was enrolled as a special constable, at the request of the proprietor, who was a strong loyalist, and that I mounted guard with a very big staff in the courtyard of Somerset House. I was myself rather afraid of the Chartists, who, down Drury-Lane way, ran large, and "would strike;" but the Altar and the Throne had to be supported, you know; and when the ominous day was safely over the proprietor treated us all to cold beef and warm ale at Betty's Chophouse. There is no Betty's Chophouse now, and the proprietor went to California.

I can't help thinking that I was a little worse off at Three Hundred and Four as Part Proprietor than I had been as Editor. In the former case I received a salary: not much, but still sufficient to keep body and soul together. In the latter case I was supposed to participate in the profits. There were no net profits, so we were constrained to appropriate the gross proceeds. Unfortunately, my co-proprietors were as hungry as I was, and on more than one occasion we were under the unpleasant necessity of fighting for the halfpence in the till. Those were the days of heavy advertisement duties:—eighteenpence on each advertisement, and cumulative penalties if you did not pay. We were always in arrear with the Stamp Office, and at one period I believe, taking all the cumulative penalties into account, we must have been indebted to her Majesty's Revenue at least One Hundred Thousand Pounds sterling. About this time, having always had a taste for speculation, I was induced to add to the publishing business the sale of the new patent medicine known as the "Shaking Quaker's Herbal Pills." They did not sell: they were not popular with the public. I'm sure I don't know why, for I took several boxes of Shaking Quakers myself, and they never did me any harm. I withdrew from the entire concern at last—quite disgusted with literature, pills, and journalism—and did not write a line for print again for three whole years.

It was not a jolly time. It was not an amusing time. During three-fourths of it I was inexpressibly wretched. I look on Three Hundred and Four now, as rapid wheels bear me daily past it, not with fond remembrance, not with a soft and mellowed interest, but with a kind of cold shuddering aversion, as a place where I suffered long and bitterly. The lessons I learned there will not, I trust, be forgotten; but any pleasure I may feel from looking back on scenes of misery arises, not from the knowledge that they were tempered by the joyousness and carelessness of youth, but by the conviction that I am better off now, and by the hope that I shall not get into such a scrape again.

The Power of Music.

"Thus it was that the enemies of Stradella, being much carried away by jealousy and all manner of wickedness, employed a certain assassin, one Rito Spalda, to kill him before he could leave the town. Stradella had gone to the Church of Sancta Capella, so that the assassin and his companion were obliged to seek him there. When they entered the sanctuary, they were immediately entranced by strains of heavenly music: their accursed hearts were struck with sorrow and very great remorse; so much so, that they flung themselves at Stradella's feet, confessing all their designs, and begging forgiveness in the name of the Holy Virgin." *Chronicles of Lombardy.*

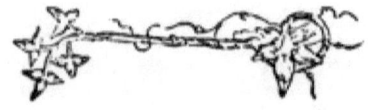

C. Morgan, del.   Dalziel Bros., sc.

THE POWER OF MUSIC.

Uncomfortable People.

By William Kirkus.

THE world swarms with uncomfortable people; and no doubt if one had only a competent knowledge of human nature, one might be able to divide this interesting tribe into dozens of genera and species. But it will be enough, and perhaps more than enough, to divide them into two grand classes — those who make themselves miserable, and those who make other people miserable. And yet it is almost too much to say that they produce misery. If a man is compelled to suffer the amputation of a limb, or even of a great-toe, there is a sort of cruel mildness in saying that he is uncomfortable; and, on the other hand, nobody but a milksop would declare that he was miserable because the dust had blown into his eyes. The discomforts of life, taken separately, are mere trifles; but unfortunately they very seldom can be taken separately. A man can have his leg amputated only once in a lifetime, but he might have it pricked with pins or worried with fleas every minute; and many people have been more frightened of mosquitoes than of an enemy in complete armour. The discomforts of life are more numerous and more incessant than great calamities, while they do not call forth the same amount of energy for their removal, or forethought for their prevention. So that uncomfortable people, though they would rather be shot than steal a silver spoon, are among the most horrible nuisances of life.

To begin with, there are the people who make *themselves* uncomfortable; and a very unaccountable folly it seems. Yet, after all, the conditions of perfect comfort are by no means superlatively easy. They are neither more nor less than these: either to be, and also to believe that you are, perfectly what you ought to be; or at any rate to believe that you are, even if you are not. Make-believe and impudence, though producing a good brassy exterior, a very safe defence against attacks from without, furnish no protection whatever against attacks from within. The cleverest liar in the world finds it uncommonly difficult to cheat his own conscience; and the most elaborate hypocrisies are precisely those which are most uncomfortable. But if a man really is everything that he ought to be, and knows that he is, there is nothing whatever to disturb him either in his own self-examination or in his dealings with other people. If they do not like him, so much the worse for them; their want of judgment in no degree embarrasses him. Indeed, so readily do our virtues degenerate into what may be called their corresponding vices, that the stupidity of our neighbours is more likely to increase than to lessen our personal comfort. But if a man knows that he is a fool, or ignorant of the ways and manners of society—if even he fancies that he is below the level of the wisdom or cleverness of those he has to do with, he is sure to be wretchedly uneasy. Even authors—people, that is to say, who have the assurance to publish to the universe their own private opinions on all manner of subjects —are far enough from being superior to the folly of this needless self-torment. With a miserable self-depreciation—which, whatever his merits may be, will reduce the market value of whatever he has done or can do by at least fifty per cent—a bashful author enters the private room of a publisher with an insane determination to sacrifice himself. To begin with, he does not like to go there at all. As long as there is the faintest excuse for not appearing in person, he contents himself with writing letters; the obvious effect of which is that half his letters are never answered at all, and the rest are snubbed. When at last he summons up courage enough to face some great lord of the book-world, he is eager to disparage his own productions, and can scarcely feel quite certain that he is not imposing on a good-natured publisher by asking him to buy a copyright. "We are very full just now," says the publisher; "and really the supply of this kind of book is so large that the market is almost glutted. The very most we can do is just to accommodate those authors whose works are most in demand; and even then we make a very slender profit." "Well, of course," says the unhappy wretch, "I can quite understand that it must be so; but still I thought that —no doubt it's an author's vanity—but I really think I have read worse books than this, and—" "Well," breaks in the publisher, "what do you want for it? and, to come to business, what's the least you'll take?" Thereupon the miserable author plunges into an abyss of self-abasement, and sells his birthright for a mess of pottage.

Idiotic ass! Now a comfortable man, a man with a firm belief in his own merits, and even his own superiority—nay, for this purpose, a man of brassy impudence, without any merits at all, or only merits of the smallest—would have managed matters with a far more lucrative result.

He would have said, " Look here, my dear boy," or old fellow, or he would have at least christiannamed or surnamed the publisher, and put himself at once on terms of easy familiarity—" look here, my dear boy, the capacious mouth of the whole universe is gaping with an insatiable hunger, which nothing but this—this little manuscript—can satisfy. Publish this, my dear boy, and you'll help to make my fortune ; and you'll very much more help to make your own. It has got wind, and I have had offers and suggestions ; but it's not in my way to desert anyone who has done *me* a good turn when I can do *him* a good turn ; so *you* shall have it, my dear boy. For this, which I will stake my reputation on affirming will be *the* book of the season, you shall just give me not a penny more (I wouldn't impose upon you) nor a penny less than—"

> " Illi robur et æs triplex
> Circa pectus erat,"

as old Horace might say of many people besides the first sailor.

Then, again, in humbler walks of life there are people who can never for the life of them be comfortable in a drawing-room. Somebody is sure to ask them to do something that they know they can't do ; or, what is far more bewildering, to do something which they know they can do, but which they think everybody else will think they can't do. There is not the slightest merit, for instance, in being able to dance, or play whist; but if you are the only person in the room who can do neither when everybody is expected to do both, you may know all about the differential and integral calculus, you may have edited half-a-dozen Greek manuscripts, and compiled a grammar of the Syriac tongue, but you'll be a very wise philosopher indeed if you don't feel an ass. Nay even in church, which ought to be so very humble a walk of life that there a man's self should simply vanish out of sight, there are hosts of people who cannot kneel down to pray without feeling uncomfortable about their legs.

"I met four or five of my old college friends in town this afternoon, my dear. They've just arrived from the country, and they are coming up here to-night to supper. Have something nice for them; not a scrap of ceremony or fudge, but enough solid stuff for five or six hungry fellows to eat. But *you* know, old girl; just make it snug and cosy."

"Well, I'm sure!" she says, "that's just like you, asking a lot of people to supper; and you know how I dislike company, and what stupids our servants are; and we have nothing nice; and I wish to goodness you'd just be a little considerate when you ask people in this way, with such short notice."

"Why, what does it matter, my dear? *they* don't care; they don't come to see me for the sake of what they can eat; and besides, the servants always do very well, and it's not a bit of extra trouble, except washing up about four more plates. It's just as easy to cook twelve or fourteen pounds of beef as it is to cook six. It hangs on the same hook, and twiddles round on the same string in front of the same fire, and—"

"Well now, come, don't you interfere. If I'm obliged to have these people, I suppose I must have them; and you just know nothing at all about it."

"Well, old girl, you needn't make a bother about it. Of course you are obliged to have them; and I'm very glad they are coming. You'll manage all right enough."

"Yes, there you go! I'm not making a bother about it at all. Of course it will be all right by my dragging myself to pieces running up and down stairs, and nearly roasting myself in front of the kitchen-fire seeing that all's right."

Now isn't it perfectly plain that the "old girl" is an uncomfortable person?

And then—not after these few only, for they are but a sample—there is scarcely a single human being who is not sticking a pin somewhere or other into his own flesh—but after the whole host of people who make *themselves* uncomfortable, there come those who make other people uncomfortable. And these are not always one's enemies, but, for instance, the people who can't keep a secret, the people who can't take a hint, the people who never understand a joke, the people who by some fatality are always asking the most inconvenient and aggravating questions. Then, again, there are the people who are always, with the best intentions, repeating every unpleasant thing they hear anybody say about you. " I was horribly vexed, my dear, and of course I contradicted it; but I think it right to let you know what is being said against you, that you may have the opportunity of contradicting it *yourself*." But unfortunately we are never able ourselves to contradict whatever any fool may choose to say about us; and as we cannot mend the mischief, it were surely just as well that we should know nothing about it.

> " Avaunt! begone! thou hast set me on the rack;
> I swear 'tis better to be much abused
> Than but to know't a little."

Once more—for amongst uncomfortable people are those who go prosing on, telling you what you know already—there are candid friends; the people who, out of the great love they bear you, must needs set all your faults and frailties full in your view, as if there were not enemies enough in the world to do that uncomfortable work for you. "What on earth is the matter with you, my dear fellow?" "O nothing—and yet there is something—there's something I want to say to you; and I don't know whether or not I ought to say it." "Why, what ever can it be? You know you are perfectly at liberty to say whatever you like to me." "Yes; but still even friends do not always like to hear of their own faults." And then he begins to say exactly what your worst enemy might have rejoiced to tell you.

And very likely I am doing the very same thing. If you'll look honestly into your own behaviour, you'll find perhaps that *you* are an uncomfortable person; and then of course I must be a very uncomfortable person for telling you so.

Love's Seasons.*

A SONG.

By William Brough.

———o———

'Twas Spring-time! I met her. To see was to
    love her;
  New hopes and new life in my heart seemed
    to rise:
All Nature looked fairer; the bright sun above her
  Shone brighter—she lent him new light from
    her eyes.

'Twas Summer! I wooed her. The corn-fields
    were turning
  To gold, as the sun his fierce rays on them
    shed;
Yet fiercer the flame in my breast that was
    burning,
  More golden the halo love shed round her
    head.

* The music for this song will be found at page 195.

'Twas Autumn! I won her. The fields, heavy-laden
   With harvest, rich joys to the reapers impart;
Yet richer *my* harvest—my own dearest maiden
   Safe housed, garnered up, in the depths of my heart.

'Tis Winter! I've lost her. All cheerless around me—
   Cold, death-like, the earth is with snow shrouded o'er;
And Despair in his cold icy fetters hath bound me;
   My young heart is frozen, to throb never more.

A Model Child.

BY E. C. BARNES.

A QUICK footstep outside my studio-door and a sharp rap roused me from my morning pipe and paper.

"Come in!" I growled, not liking the interruption, for I was just in the middle of an interesting paragraph, "Starved to death in London;" and trying to twist it into a sensation-picture for the next Academy. The door opened with a jerk, and the first thing I saw was a large ragged umbrella, the rain streaming in a long silver thread from the stumpy ferule; then followed a strange, careworn little face, surrounded with shaggy black hair, that looked as if it had stopped growing, all the ends having made frantic efforts to curl, and given it up as a failure. The different locks

A "MODEL" CHILD.

had evidently not kept pace with each other, for
they were all manner of lengths, straggling about,
and very wet; one wisp falling from under the old
speckled-straw hat, and across her pale cheek,
gave a notion that it was a large note of exclamation on a clean sheet of paper. On her shoulders
she wore an old-fashioned black-silk cape, trimmed
with heavy fringe that reached below her knees;
the rest of her wardrobe was of the scantiest description, old, but clean.

"Hallo! how are yer? ain't I jolly wet!" was
the first greeting, spoken in a thick voice, as though
some old cold was struggling with the words in her
throat and getting the best of it; then after cast-
ing her eyes—a bright and knowing pair!—
rapidly round the room, she said, "Can yer give
me a sitting to-day?"

"Why, Sally, you little imp! what's brought
you out such a day as this?"

"Why, you see, mother has gone to rehearsal.
She's in the pantomime at Ashley's this year;
she's going to play Queen Bright-eyes; ain't it a
lark to call her Bright-eyes, when one of hers is
a glass un! But I tell her nobody 'll see it from
the front of the house. She does some dancing as
well. I should have been with her, only we can't
both leave Francis Henry."

"Why, who is he?" I asked.

"He's my little brother, you know; him as

you painted when he had the tooth-rash, and you said he did very well for a saint; he's a dear little chap, he is; he's the only comfort I've got. Well, after mother had gone out, I tidied up a bit, swept our room—you know, I do all the house-work,—then I gave Francis Henry his cold potato."

" His what ?"

" His cold potato; he always has one when I go out, to play with. Then he eats it. Lor bless you! with that and a few cinders he'll sit as good as good for hours together. He's got a doll—it's the first we've had in the family; I bought it with one of the pennies that gentleman gave me—your friend—him with the carroty beard, as looks so miserable, and says such funny things; with the other copper I bought a reel of cotton for mother, and a ha'p'orth of sweets for me and Francis Henry. He's such a dear; he did swallow 'em up quick. I give Kitty Mathews some to come and stop with him a bit, and she lent me her umbrella; it ain't a very good un, is it?"

" No," I answered; " I shouldn't be proud of it."

"O, I don't mind; it ain't many people as looks at me: and I wanted to come and see if you could give me a sitting."

" I'm afraid not to-day," I replied.

"Then I must cut it, and earn a shilling or two somewhere, for next week is Christmas, and Charley 'll be coming back. I mean to have a good plum-pudding this year; we had a very small one last, only the size of a dumpling; for what with father dying, and Charley going away, we couldn't manage it. But there, if father had been alive he wouldn't have helped us much. Ah, he was a bad un to poor mother and me! He starved us all for his drink. Why, the very day he died, he told mother to send me out to see if any of the artists wished to paint a dying man, for he wanted some more rum! Wasn't it awful?"

"Yes," I said, while humming to myself,

"Thy gentle voice still leads me on,
My own, my guiding star."

"He was a nice man; he ought to have been painted. It's a good job he's dead," she went on. "Francis Henry won't hear any swearing, nor see his mother kicked, as I used to. I got the little pudding I was telling you about, last Christmas, by playing one of my father's tricks. Mother was very down and fretting about Charley, so I thought it would do her good and cheer her up a bit; but there wasn't many currants in it. I'll tell you how it was. We hadn't any money; so I persuaded mother to pawn my boots. My father always did if he got a chance. I've lost lots of sittings by it. They were quite new, and I wasn't going to any studios; all the artists were gone away enjoying themselves, and it didn't matter about my going out of doors for a few days. We had dinner all to ourselves. I think I eat it nearly all. Mother was mending her dancing-shoes, and crying about my brother. But he's coming back next week, and we shall have a jolly lark! I've saved up two shillings unbeknown to mother!"

"Don't wink at me, you little wretch," I said; "but give me a light for my pipe, and tell me where's Charley been to all the year?"

The little creature's expression suddenly changed, and pausing in the act of lighting a piece of paper, walked close up to my elbow, and with a mysterious nod towards the lay figure, as though she doubted that that object's sense of honour would not prevent its listening, whispered, "I don't know for certain, but I've my suspicions —and I think I'm right—he's in prison!"

Her face now wore a sad and troubled look that was very touching. I hope I may not often see so little of the child left in a child. She was only ten years of age, but she looked twenty.

"How do you think I found it out," she continued. "You know we live up at Clerkenwell, in one of those holes they call courts. Well, every day when I went home from sitting, if mother was with me, she would send me on first to open the door, and she was always a long time following me. One day—it was raining like it is now—I was going home from here; just as I turned the corner by the pawnshop, who should I see leaning against the prison-wall but mother! I knowed she was a-crying, she shook so; I'd seen her too often when father was alive not to know that. She was leaning, with her face covered in her shawl, against the cold bricks, and tapping on the wall with the door-key. Just as I was going to speak, I heard her sob out, so pitifully, so pitifully! 'O Charley, Charley! poor soul, poor soul! I know *you* didn't do it; I always said it wasn't *you! He* told the truth before he died. God forgive him for *your* sufferings, my poor boy, my true heart!' When I heard that, I went home; but I never said anything to her about it, and Charley shall never know what I heard as long as ever I live. Mother would be worse if she thought I knew. But, my eye! ain't I wasting my time! You don't want me to sit, then?"

"No, my dear, not to-day. The picture is finished. Some other time."

How the Ghost Walked.

BY HENRY LESLIE.

———o———

SOME years ago a popular actor (a son of one still more famous) was, while still engaged in London, also the lessee of a small provincial theatre within a few miles' distance of the metropolis. The public of the little town looked coldly on his speculation. In the course of the season business drooped from bad to worse, till, the managerial capital being exhausted, the payments from the treasury became uncertain; ultimately, indeed, the only reliance the "poor players" had for their Sunday meal was on the rather handsome salary received by the manager for his histrionic displays in London, and which he forwarded with the most honourable regularity to his actors in the country.

In most travelling companies there are one or two individuals noticeable for some oddity of character or peculiarity of temperament. In this particular one, the "old man" was a leading eccentricity. He took a singular pride in a chronic state of ill-health, to which he declared himself a martyr, and which, in his opinion, entitled him to dictate to any other person who might be suffering from the slightest indisposition. A cough from the merest stranger would be a sufficient inducement for him to take a medical work — which, apart from his profession, was his only study — out of his pocket, and read to that stranger whole pages of the probable inconveniences or fatal results which might press closely on the heels of his slight catarrh. By these means he contrived, with the best intentions, to make everybody by turns intensely miserable around him. Another peculiarity of the same man was his habit of putting people down by the most daring, but not always truthful, assertions. Thus, if the conversation turned upon some point of church-discipline, he would declare that he was thoroughly acquainted with the subject, because he had taken orders. If the topic were the army, he would say he had held her Majesty's commission; if the law, that he had been called to the bar; and so on.

Advantage was once taken of this habit to play a practical joke upon him, which he never entirely forgave.

One evening, in his presence, the conversation

was artfully turned on law points, as connected with the conduct of criminal trials at the Old Bailey. One of the company roundly expressed a positive disbelief that there were any persons base enough to perjure themselves for money considerations. Everyone coincided loudly in this belief except our belligerent old man. "Pooh, pooh! nonsense!—you know nothing!" he said. "Thing is of every-day occurrence. I've done it myself often."

Another oddity in the same company was an American actor, who had positively travelled from the States to this country on the strength of one joke. This was the joke: in cheap-John fashion he would profess to be selling a pill, and in recommendation would cite an instance of the father of a family taking one for the gout, which not only cured him completely, but also relieved his wife from the rheumatism, his children from the measles, and besides all this, to the profound astonishment of everybody, mended the kitchen-stairs. Feeble as the joke originally was, it became still more attenuated by frequent repetition, till at last the poor fellow was obliged to do almost anything to earn a scant, irregularly-paid salary. This "funny" actor's properties consisted only of a lace collar, a pair of ribbon rosettes, and a paste buckle. Handy at his needle, he had made a small bag to contain these, and thus protect them from damage or loss. Once, while out walking with a fellow-actor some distance from the town, he was informed by his companion that an execution for rent was threatened in the house where he lodged.

"Well, they can't touch me," replied the American.

"But they can seize your wardrobe, though."

The moment this was made clear to him, he started off at the top of his speed.

"Hullo, where are you going?" shouted his friend, panting after him in pursuit.

"Home," responded the Yankee, "home: there's all my property hanging on the window-shutter!"

A third character was a stout old scene-painter, who, despite a lisp, had, by the exigencies of the business, occasionally to appear on the stage. On these occasions he was regularly hissed by the few little boys who patronised the gallery. One evening he was cast for the Uncle in "Lillo's sublime tragedy" of *George Barnwell*. The moment he made his appearance he was, as usual, received with marks of disapprobation.

"Beatht of boyth!" exclaimed the Uncle. "You might have waited till I thpoke." He then went on, in the words of the "sublime dramatist" aforesaid, "If I were thuperthitouth, I thould fear that death were nigh, or thome danger were at hand," &c.

When he got to the end of his speech, he waited quietly to be shot by his nephew, who ought to have been lurking behind. The Uncle turned round, and caught a glimpse of him at the wings.

"Come and thoot me!" roared the Uncle.

"Can't find the pistol," whispered the anxious Barnwell at the wings.

"Thtab me!" said the Uncle.

"All right; I've got it," whispered Barnwell.

Uncle returned to his former place on the stage, and, without the least expression in his countenance, waited to be shot. He heard his nephew behind, snapping the pistol, but no explosion followed. The weapon was not loaded. The painter, however, was fertile in expedients. Stimulated by the titters of the small audience, he rushed up to Barnwell, took the pistol, placed the empty barrel to his forehead, and shouting out the single word "bang!" fell in the convulsive agonies of death, amid the unrestrained merriment of both audience and actors.

The foregoing were three members of a company who one Saturday evening—for in those times there was no performance on the Saturday—were waiting most anxiously for the "ghost" (that is, the salary), which it was hoped would "walk" on that, the seventh, day of the week.

The messenger, who up to that particular date

had regularly arrived from our manager in London, put in no appearance on this occasion; and his non-arrival, as may be supposed, filled the hearts of the expectant actors with the utmost dismay. It was the first time they had been thus disappointed, and the situation was in reality most distressing. Their discomfort was the more painful from its contrast with the easy jollity of the leader of the band, who, by a simple but most effectual expedient, invariably contrived to obtain his nightly stipend in advance. Doubtful of the resources of the treasury, he regularly impawned his violin with a good-natured publican for the precise amount of his nightly "screw;" and as without his fiddle there could be no music, the instrument had to be redeemed from the amount of the first slender receipts of the theatre, in order that the promise of the play-bill might be fulfilled, and that there should be an "overture by the band."

The last boat from London had arrived; there would be no train until nearly midnight, and still the company were waiting on the stage for that "ghost" which it seemed most unlikely would perambulate that night. Member gazed upon member with glances of blank discouragement, till suddenly the face of our low comedian lighted up with hope, as his eye fell on a something quietly reposing in one corner of the orchestra.

Now this something was an enormous double-bass, which looked almost offensively fat and comfortable in its voluminous wrapper of green baize.

The owner of this instrument was a watchmaker in the town, who was supposed to add to the profits of his business in the day by the exercise of his musical abilities at night.

"Hem!" coughed the low comedian.

"Hem!" chorussed the rest of the company.

"How much, eh?" demanded the low comedian, in a semi-jocular manner, of the leader, jerking his left thumb over his shoulder.

"About thirty bob," replied the experienced musician.

There was, for a few moments, a pause of consideration.

Thirty shillings divided amongst them would be nearly half-a-crown each, sufficient to provide at least a chop and a loaf for the Sunday.

"*Do* it!" exclaimed the leader, breaking in upon the deliberation. The temptation proved too strong—they *did* it.

The double-bass was placed over the shoulder of a "general utility," who, attended by the rest of his fellows in order to "see fair," marched with his burden down the High-street and up a narrow alley, where the only pawnbroker then in the town had a private entrance for the accommodation of his customers.

It being Saturday night, the majority of the

regular customers of "my uncle" were taking their household gods out, and consequently it was with the greatest difficulty that the actors with their gigantic charge could force their way in. At last, by a series of vigorous efforts, the object was accomplished, and the huge instrument safely deposited on the pawnbroker's counter.

Not till the self-elected spokesman found himself face to face with the shopman did he realise the criminal nature of the proceeding in which he was a principal party. Paralysed with fear, he became pale and speechless. The whole design would have at once collapsed had not one of the party, more bold and unscrupulous, shouted, "Thirty shillings!" The sum asked was advanced, and duly divided amongst the company.

Wrong this, undoubtedly; but the repentance, the agony of remorse, which, *after the money was spent*, descended on each party to the transaction, was pitiable to witness. Their only hope was in the speedy arrival of the manager or his messenger, and the consequent redemption of the double-bass before its absence should be discovered by its proprietor.

The Sunday passed without any sign of the coming of either. The terrors of penal servitude were discussed in secret conclave. Indeed, had any money been left at all, the catastrophe of a discovery would have been avoided by a general departure of the company from the town. Monday morning—no manager, no messenger; and, horror upon horror, a full-band rehearsal! What would the respectable old watchmaker say, when, entering the orchestra, he looked for his double-bass in vain? At one time it was considered rather a good plan to bolt every door of the theatre, and barricade him out altogether. This idea, however, was necessarily dismissed by the too early arrival of the watchmaker himself. A glimpse of his bald head was sufficient. The stage was cleared in a moment, the company watching from various dark recesses what effect the discovery of his loss would create on the respectable old watchmaker.

For an instant or two his astonishment seemed to deprive him of sense; he searched for his double-bass even under the music-stools and in other impossible places; he wandered about the theatre; but as everybody who knew anything about it kept most religiously out of the way, he could of course glean no information. Finally, he sat down bewildered. It was at last agreed by the company that the mortgage-ticket should be enclosed in an envelope, and delivered to him by an " innocent party."

Fortunately for the company, the rage of the watchmaker was checked by the welcome appearance of the manager on the stage, who, when he heard the circumstances, gave a light-comedy tone to the affair; and the double-bass being once more placed in the orchestra, the evil results that might otherwise have happened were avoided.

"What foolish fellows you all were!" said the good-natured watchmaker a few days afterwards; "if you had dropped round at my shop, I'd have lent you thirty shillings with pleasure."

Buckingham Gate.

———o———

ABOUT a century prior to the ever-memorable year 1666, which saw its complete demolition, old Saint Paul's Cathedral was partially destroyed by fire. The reëdification of the cathedral lagged for want of funds, and a portion of the stone which had been provided for its restoration was "borrowed" by the first Duke of Buckingham, who built with it the now interesting architectural relic of old London which stands at the bottom of Buckingham-street, Strand. It marks the site of York House, celebrated as having been successively the residence of the Archbishops of York, the birthplace of Francis Bacon—"the greatest, brightest, meanest of mankind"—and the home of one who with even more truth has been called "the profligate and time-serving Villiers."

The gate was erected in 1636 by Inigo Jones;

J. O'Connor, del.   Dalziel Bros., sc.

BUCKINGHAM GATE.

and we need hardly add that it is the only vestige remaining of the once splendid mansion to which it was the water-entrance. Buckingham Gate is executed in rock-work or rustic, in the Italian style of architecture, the material being Portland stone. It is justly regarded as a very tasteful and appropriate structure of its kind. The front of the arch facing the river bears the arms of the Villiers family; and on the north front is inscribed their family motto, "*Fidei corticula crux*, the cross is the touchstone of faith." Time, however, has to a great extent defaced its outlines and obliterated its ornamentation.

"There is not," says a recent writer, "connected with the biography of genius, a more solemn spot than the vicinity of Buckingham Gate. It was the scene of one of the most mournful tragedies in the moral life of the human race. There is an interest here surpassing aught that belongs to the homes of Newton, Milton, or Cromwell, the cottage in which Shakespeare was born, or the cottage in which Burns died. There is a mournfulness of local association connected with the site of York House far surpassing in deep sadness anything which invests the dungeon of Tasso;" for here Bacon was born, celebrated, and disgraced. But there are pleasant associations as well. Peter the Great lived in a house (Pepys's) on the site of the last house on the west side of the street. The studio of William Etty the painter was in the same street; and who but remembers that Mrs. Crupp, the landlady of David Copperfield, lived in Buckingham-street, Strand? The important improvements now in progress in connection with the Thames Embankment are at this moment sweeping away Buckingham Gate. What will become of it remains to be seen.

The End.

LONDON:
DOBSON AND SON, GREAT NORTHERN PRINTING WORKS,
PANCRAS ROAD, N.W.

www.ingramcontent.com/pod-product-compliance
Lightning Source LLC
Chambersburg PA
CBHW030323240426
43673CB00040B/1258